The Polar Bear

Master of the Ice

Text by Valerie Tracqui

READER'S DIGEST
Animal Close-Ups

This edition is published by Reader's Digest Young Families, Inc.
Pleasantville, NY 10570
www.readersdigest.com

Copyright © Éditions Milan 1991. Toulouse, France.
Original edition first published by Éditions Milan under the title *l'ours blanc, seigneur de la banquise*
French series editor, Valérie Tracqui
Translated by Boston Language Institute

Copyright © 1994 in USA by Charlesbridge Publishing, Watertown, MA .

cover photo "© Alaska Stock/Tom Soucek 1999"

This huge male polar bear weighs almost 1,100 pounds. Its long, cat-like claws and strong sharp teeth are signs that it is a carnivore, a meat eater. It is the largest land carnivore in the world.

Endless winter

A storm howls. Great gusts of wind blow over a landscape of ice and snow. Near the North Pole, in the area called the Arctic Circle, the sun never actually rises during late winter. The temperature goes down to 40° below zero, and the silvery ice seems to join with the sky.

In the distance, the huge shape of a polar bear appears like a ghost through the mists. Tired after its long trek, it stops to rest. Then, it moves on again southward, over the frozen sea. At times, the huge bear runs along at a speed of nearly 25 miles an hour. It roams a vast territory in search of food.

Ready for the cold

Even in the freezing wind, the huge polar bear is perfectly comfortable. The long, white hairs of its thick fur let the sunlight pass right through them. This special type of fur lets the warmth of the sun reach the bear's black skin. The blinding glare of the sun on the white snow is not a problem for a polar bear. Its eyes are specially adapted to work like sunglasses and screen out the glare.

Its huge paws are as big as dinnerplates. The bottoms of the paws are insulated from the cold by short, stiff hairs that form a non-slip pad. Each toe has a long, black claw as sharp as an ice pick.

Polar bears have good balance. They can stand on their hind legs to look around or sniff the air.

Today, a heavy storm has made it difficult to find food, so the polar bear digs itself a shelter. It will stop to sleep for a few days.

Heavy, long, thick fur and a 4 inch layer of fat under its skin are very good protection from the cold.

Other adaptations are small ears that lose very little heat and no eyelashes which would freeze in icy storms.

The bottoms of its big, furry feet are like natural snowshoes. The polar bear does not need to worry about slipping on the ice.

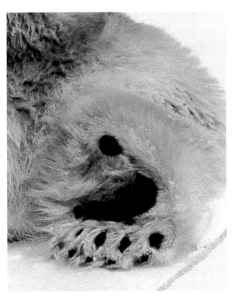

Very patiently, a polar
bear waits for hours
near a hole in the ice.
Perhaps a seal will come
up for air.

A seal weighing
over 50 pounds
would make a
good meal for a
polar bear.

This Arctic fox has followed the polar bear to find and eat any food the bear leaves behind.

Hunting for seals

For five days the polar bear has not eaten, and it is very hungry. Suddenly it stops, its black nose twitching. It turns its head from side to side, catching the scent of a seal miles away. The hunt begins.

The polar bear climbs onto a floating piece of ice and then silently slips into the water, causing hardly a ripple. Between each piece of ice, it swims underwater. Each time it comes to the surface to breathe, it is a little closer to the seal. Suddenly, it comes up right beside the sleeping seal. With a single swipe of its paw, the hunt is over.

In the water, a seal can swim too fast for a polar bear to catch. Polar bears need to catch about one seal a week.

A swimming champion

As winter comes to an end, the ice begins to break up. The polar bear does not worry about floating out to sea. It can swim for miles if it needs to. It can hold its breath underwater for several minutes, and its partly webbed paws make it a fast swimmer. When it decides to climb out onto the ice, it grips the ice with its sharp claws, using them like steel hooks.

When a wet polar bear hauls itself out of the water, it is a strange sight. Its narrow head, nine-foot-long body and small tail give it a streamlined shape for swimming.

In the water, the longer hairs of the polar bear's fur keep the thick fur beneath dry.

When swimming underwater, the polar bear closes its nostrils but keeps its eyes open.

When the polar bear climbs out of the icy water, it shakes like a dog. The water runs out of its fur before it freezes.

Two baby bears

On a beautiful sunny day in March, two four-month-old polar bears come outdoors for the first time.

They were born in a den their mother dug in the snow. There they were sheltered from the wind and the cold. When spring arrived, the mother bear used her paws like snow shovels to reopen the tunnel doorway.

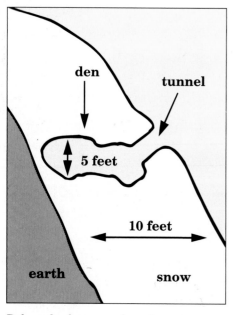

Baby polar bears are born in a snow cave called a den.

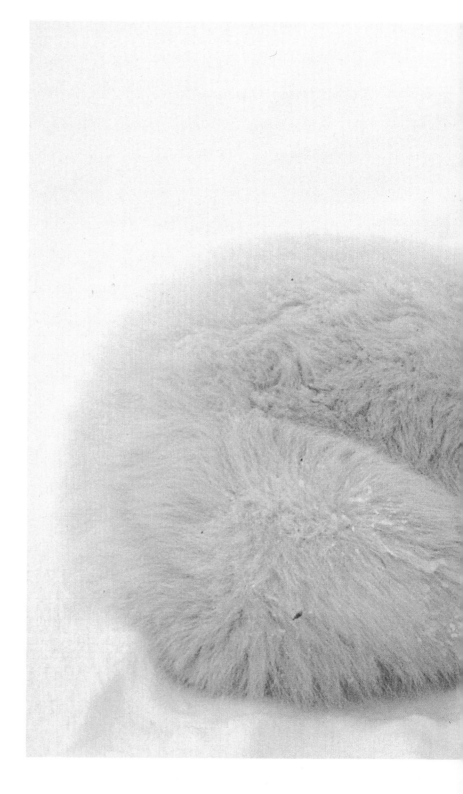

The mother polar bear did not sleep all winter. She hibernated by slowing down her breathing and dozing for about five months. Her heart beat slowed down, but her body temperature changed very little. She did not need to eat during her long nap because her layer of fat was her source of food.

In December, the mother polar bear gave birth to two tiny cubs. Newborn polar bear cubs weigh about as much as kittens, and like newborn kittens, their eyes are not open.

After a month, the cubs' eyes were open. They spent their days snuggling up against their mother for warmth and drinking her milk.

When they finally leave the den, the cubs weigh about 20 to 30 pounds.

13

The polar bear cubs drink their mother's milk until they are one and a half years old. The cubs will stay with their mother until they are two years old.

Each day, the mother takes her cubs out to explore. There is much to see and many lessons to learn.

Always playful, the cubs often frolic with their mother. Each night, they return to the safety of their den.

During the spring, the family begins a long trip across the ice.

Family life

The curious cubs watch carefully everything their mother does. They play games together, rolling, climbing, and sliding on the snow. After a few weeks, the mother is so hungry that she must leave the den and head for the seal-hunting grounds.

The cubs bravely follow their mother across miles of ice. The mother stops often so her babies can have a drink and take a nap. She sniffs the air for the smell of danger. Prowling wolf packs look for easy prey such as bear cubs. For the moment, everything is fine. The mother gives a few grunts to tell the cubs that it is time to move on.

Water games

After they learn how to swim, polar bears love to play in the water. Even on their first day in the water, they begin to play games that test their strength and develop their coordination.

Although they will rarely fight when they are grown, young bears often play by pretending to fight each other.

The playmates are careful not to hurt each other.

Each one tries to splash and knock down the other cub.

The bigger the cubs get, the more fun their water sports become. These two have rolled off the ice into the water!

Roaring and hissing and showing your teeth — all part of the game.

Slowly turning together in the water, one cub nips at his sister's nose. She kicks her brother away. Then they give each other a big bear hug!

A brief encounter

It is now May, the time when male and female polar bears meet to mate. Drawn by her scent, two males approach a female. This female has no cubs to care for.

The two males lower their heads menacingly and turn to face each other. Then the contest begins. With the hair on their backs standing straight up, they begin circling each other, grunting out warnings. They wrestle until the weaker of the two acknowledges the strength of his rival and leaves. The winner will spend only about a week with the female before he leaves to hunt for food.

Standing on his hind legs, a male polar bear is tall enough to look an elephant in the eye. He may weigh as much as 1,500 pounds.

Polar bear mothers take care of their cubs for two years. The mother can have a new pair of cubs every 3 years.

18

When mating time is over, the males go off to live alone. They will not be able to recognize their own cubs if they should ever meet them.

Mother polar bear teaches her cubs how to hunt small rodents, called lemmings.

Hungry polar bears will eat moss, lichen, leaves, and berries.

Even though white fur in the snow is excellent camouflage, the arctic hare cannot hide from a polar bear's powerful sense of smell.

Polar bears like to stay clean. After eating, mother bear shows her cubs the proper way to use one's paws to wash, just like a cat.

On the tundra

Summer is coming. The sun looks like a big red circle on the horizon. The ice is breaking up into pieces that drift out to sea. Mother bear must either lead her cubs north, following the seals, or teach the cubs how to get food on the tundra. She chooses the tundra.

In summer on the tundra, polar bears become omnivores, eating anything they can find. They eat bird eggs and hatchlings, fish, rodents, lichen, seaweed, and berries. Frequent plunges in the nearby water help them to cool off.

Young Arctic foxes wait for the polar bear's leftovers.

The cubs grow up

After two months on the tundra, mother polar bear knows that soon winter will begin. The first sign is ice around the edge of the bay. Then the waters freeze and again become a solid sheet of ice. At last, the seals return.

This winter the mother and her cubs do not stay in a den. They hunt seals all winter. They curl up together during storms and let the falling snow be their blanket. In the spring, the mother says goodbye to the cubs, and they go off on their own. They do not need her help and protection anymore.

The cubs are two years old when they leave their mother. They stay together for a few weeks before they decide to leave each other, too.

Polar bears and people

For two hundred years, polar bears were killed for their fur. Today they're protected by an international treaty. Slowly, their numbers have increased, but now a new menace threatens their safety: pollution.

In trying to find food in the autumn, polar bears sometimes visit dumps, where they may be harmed by eating poisonous chemicals.

An Inuit spirit
For thousands of years, the Inuit (Eskimos) worshipped the polar bear as a spirit. It was bad luck to anger "Nanouk," as the Inuit called the bear spirit. They hunted the polar bear with great skill. They ate its meat and used its fur to make parkas, shoes, and leggings.

Hunted for 200 years
It is thought that polar bears lived in the Arctic for fifty to eighty thousand years before the arrival of the first whaling vessels in the 1600's. Then, for the next two hundred years, non-native hunters brought guns to the Arctic and killed thousands of polar bears each year. The bears were killed only for their fur and for sport.

Protected at last
Finally, international cooperation was necessary to adequately protect this endangered species. In 1965, every nation bordering the arctic decided to ban the hunting of polar bear mothers and their cubs. The polar bear is still on the international list of endangered species.

In order to study a polar bear, scientists first tranquilize it so they can weigh and examine it.

At the crossroads

In 1974, a treaty was signed by the five countries bordering the Arctic. It banned the capture of polar bears, except by scientists working to preserve the species, and by Inuit, who are allowed to hunt only a certain number every year.

Five nations are involved with the protection of polar bears.

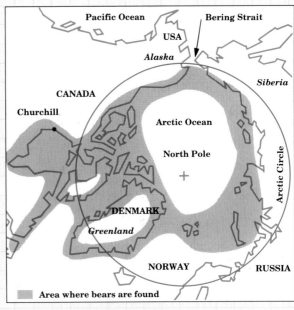

A map of polar bear territory

Each year, the Inuit are allowed to hunt some polar bears in Alaska and some in Greenland.

Game preserves

The treaty of 1976 called for the five nations to protect the polar bear's feeding and breeding grounds and their migration routes. Today, the polar bear population is slowly recovering. In certain areas where polar bears are plentiful, a thriving tourist industry has arisen. The town of Churchill, Manitoba on Hudson Bay, has become "the polar bear capital of Canada."

The pollution threat

Even if there isn't much risk of being hunted anymore, polar bears still face another threat: pollution. Researchers have found pesticides and dangerous metals in the bodies of both polar bears and seals. Increasing development of natural resources such as oil also threaten their fragile environment. A single oil tanker accident could have catastrophic consequences.

Other kinds of bears

The bear family includes seven species. The three largest are the brown bear, the black bear and the polar bear. These three bears are the largest carnivores on the face of the earth.

The American Black Bear includes 18 sub-species which have a variety of colors. It is smaller than the brown bear and has shorter hair and claws. The claws are sharp enough to quickly climb trees. More timid than the brown bear and native to a wider geographic area, it usually doesn't bother people.

The European Brown Bear lives in forests, plains and mountains and is a good tree climber. It usually hunts at night. Because there are only a few left in France, there is a real danger that this bear might disappear entirely. Brown bears are protected by law, but they suffer from battles with wild pigs, a shrinking forest, and the growing presence of tourists.

▼

◄ The Grizzly Bear is an American sub-species of brown bear. Larger than its European cousin, it is quite impressive when rearing up on its hind legs to better observe an unfamiliar object or person. It can be found in national parks where it is protected and in less developed parts of Canada and Alaska. Along the rivers, grizzlies fish for salmon. Sometimes several grizzlies can be seen in the same area fishing.

For Further Reading...

Horton, Casey. *Endangered! Bears*. New York: Marshall Cavendish, 1996.

Lepthien, Emilie. *Polar Bears*. A New True Book. Chicago: Childrens Press, 1991.

Matthews, Downs. *Polar Bear Cubs*. Photographs by Dan Guravich. New York: Simon and Schuster Books for Young Readers, 1989.

To See Polar Bears in Captivity...

Many zoos also have web sites on the internet. To learn more about their exhibits, go to the following page on the Yahoo WWW site:
> **http://www.yahoo.com/science/biology/zoology/zoos**

Use the Internet to Find Out More About Polar Bears...

Seaworld / Busch Gardens: Polar Bears. Lots of information with a great index.
> **http://www/seaworld.org/polar_bears/pbindex.html**

Polar Bears Alive. A great photo gallery.
> **http://www.polarbearsalive.org/gallery.htm**

Zoobooks. Pet a polar bear!
> **http://www.zoobooks.com/petp.htm**

The Polar Bear and the Walrus. Make a blubber mitten.
> **http://www.teelfamily.com/activities/polarbear/**

2500
fascinating
FACTS

Written by
Rupert Matthews, Gerald Legg,
Moira Butterfield, Chris Oxlade and Jon Day

Edited by
Paul Harrison, Kay Barnham, Philippa Moyle,
Nicola Wright, Hazel Songhurst and Fiona Mitchell

SCHOLASTIC INC.
New York Toronto London Auckland Sydney

CONTENTS

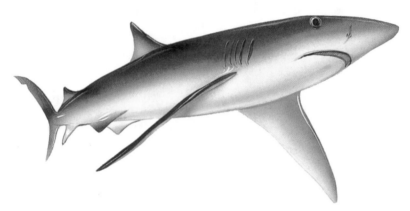

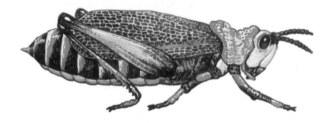

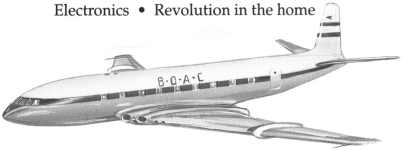

Coral creatures

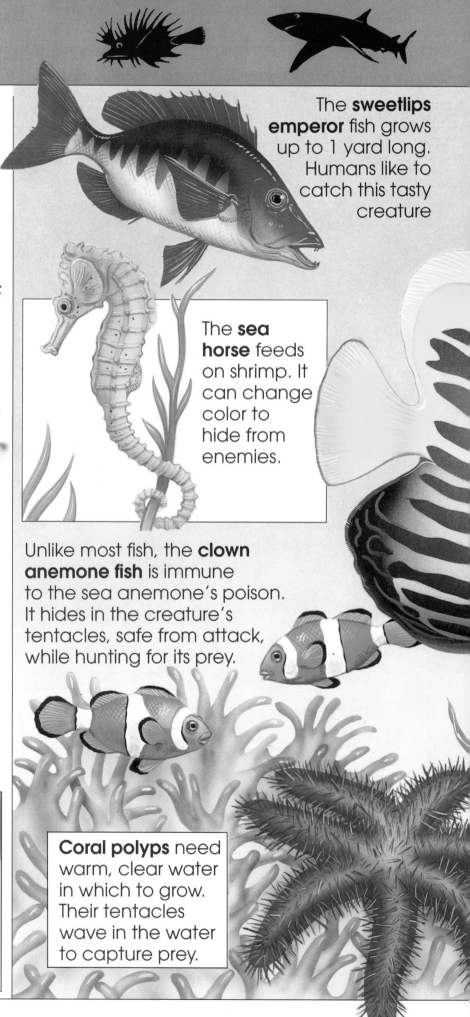

Coral reefs are made from millions of tiny creatures called coral polyps. When it dies, each polyp leaves behind a tiny limestone skeleton. There are thousands of types of polyp.

Many other creatures live on the reef. The shallow water and rocky crevices provide an ideal home.

The largest coral reef in the world is the **Great Barrier Reef** off the east coast of Queensland, Australia. It is over 1,243 mi. long.

The **sweetlips emperor** fish grows up to 1 yard long. Humans like to catch this tasty creature

The **sea horse** feeds on shrimp. It can change color to hide from enemies.

Unlike most fish, the **clown anemone fish** is immune to the sea anemone's poison. It hides in the creature's tentacles, safe from attack, while hunting for its prey.

Coral polyps need warm, clear water in which to grow. Their tentacles wave in the water to capture prey.

The **blue shark** cruises the reef, hunting for prey.

The **imperial angelfish** has bright stripes to match the colors of the coral.

A **lionfish** has bright stripes to warn other fish that its spines are poisonous.

The **stonefish** looks like a stone and hides in gaps in the reef. Any human who steps on its poisonous spines would die!

Anemones use their tentacles to catch prey. Poisonous barbs kill the fish which are then pulled into the anemone's mouth.

The **crown of thorns starfish** eats coral polyps. Usually, new polyps replace those eaten and the reef survives any damage.

5

Life on the shore can be very difficult for animals. As the tide comes in and goes out, their surroundings change from dry land to shallow sea.

Pounding waves throw animals around. The sand is always moving as the sea pushes and pulls it around. Seashore animals must be tough to survive.

Shrimp feed among the seaweed. When the tide goes out, they swim into deeper water, but sometimes they are caught in rock pools.

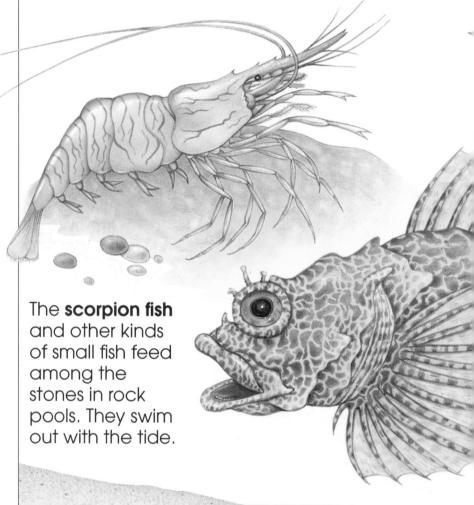

The **scorpion fish** and other kinds of small fish feed among the stones in rock pools. They swim out with the tide.

The **masked crab** lives on sandy beaches. When the tide goes out, it burrows into the sand. The tips of its two antennae poke out of the sand and act as breathing tubes.

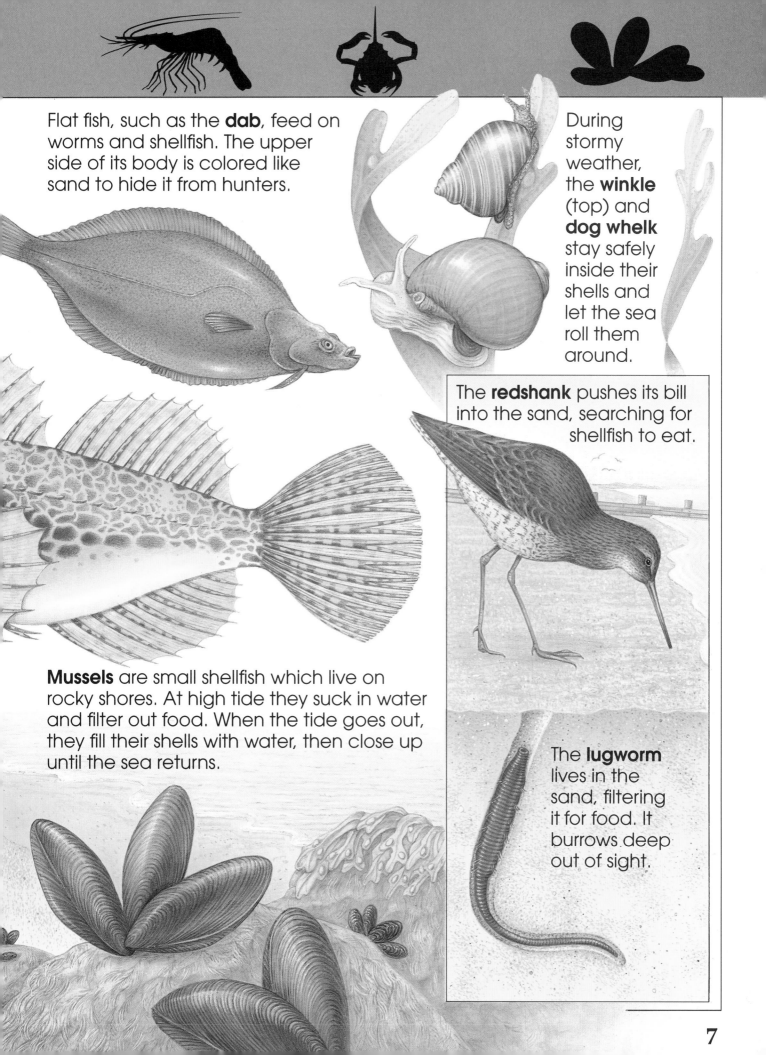

Flat fish, such as the **dab**, feed on worms and shellfish. The upper side of its body is colored like sand to hide it from hunters.

During stormy weather, the **winkle** (top) and **dog whelk** stay safely inside their shells and let the sea roll them around.

The **redshank** pushes its bill into the sand, searching for shellfish to eat.

Mussels are small shellfish which live on rocky shores. At high tide they suck in water and filter out food. When the tide goes out, they fill their shells with water, then close up until the sea returns.

The **lugworm** lives in the sand, filtering it for food. It burrows deep out of sight.

Deep-sea creatures

Most sea creatures live near the surface, where the water is warm and sunlit. The light cannot travel very deep and the sea's currents rarely move the warm surface water down to the depths of the ocean.

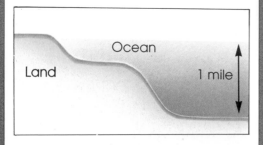

Ocean

Land

1 mile

At depths of more than 1 mile, the sea is very cold and completely dark. Some very strange creatures live here. They feed on each other and on food which drifts down from above.

Sperm whales dive down for food.

The **giant squid** can grow to 65 feet long.

Deep-sea shrimp can glow to attract a mate.

The **deep-sea angler fish** has a long growth over its mouth which glows faintly. This attracts other fish, which are then swallowed whole!

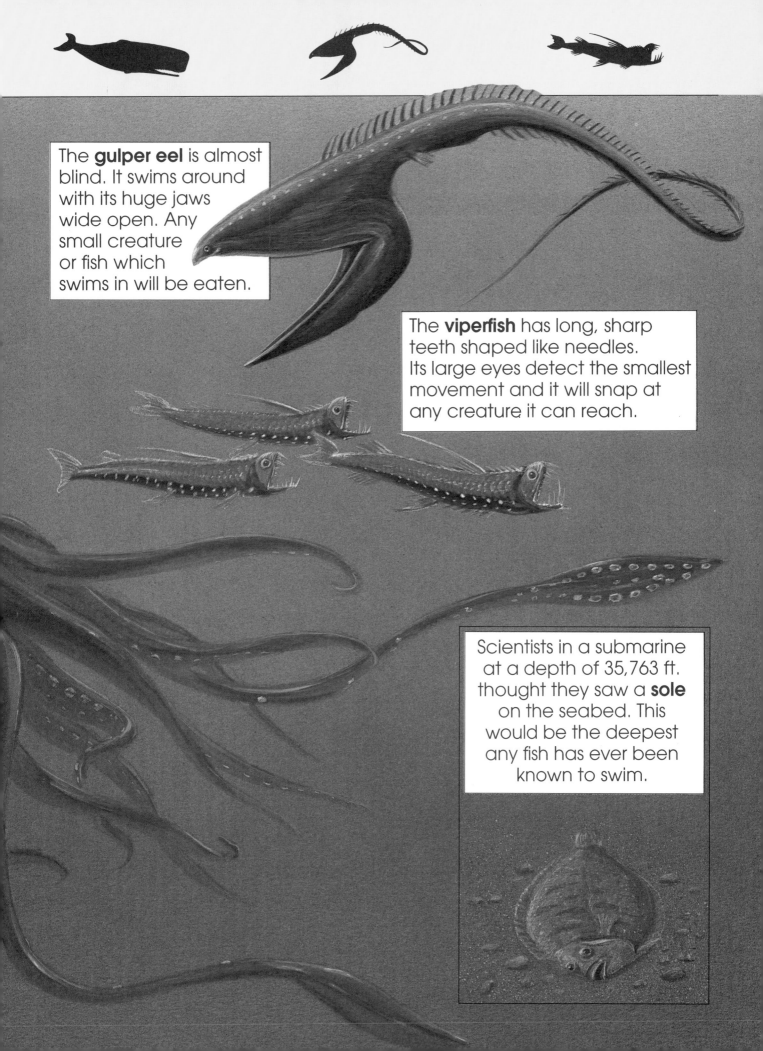

The **gulper eel** is almost blind. It swims around with its huge jaws wide open. Any small creature or fish which swims in will be eaten.

The **viperfish** has long, sharp teeth shaped like needles. Its large eyes detect the smallest movement and it will snap at any creature it can reach.

Scientists in a submarine at a depth of 35,763 ft. thought they saw a **sole** on the seabed. This would be the deepest any fish has ever been known to swim.

Around both the North and South Poles, the weather is very cold. A layer of ice floats on top of the sea all year round.

Animals which live there must be able to keep warm. They may have thick fur, like the polar bear, or layers of fat under their skin, like the common seal.

Killer whales prey on any creatures they can catch. They will even push ice from underwater to knock penguins and seals into the sea.

Penguins are birds that live around the South Pole. They lay their eggs on the ice and hunt for fish in the sea.

The largest penguin is the **Emperor penguin** which grows to over 3 feet tall.

The smallest penguin is the **fairy penguin**, which is only 16 in. tall.

Seals live in the oceans around the North and South Poles. The **gray seal** grows up to 7.8 ft. long. The **common seal** hunts for fish and squid in northern waters. The fierce **leopard seal** from the southern oceans hunts penguins as well as fish.

Gray seal

Common seal

Leopard seal

Cod

Haddock

Squid

Plankton

Polar bears live on the northern ice where they hunt seals, snow hares and other animals.

Beneath the ice live large numbers of **squid** and fish such as **cod** and **haddock**. They feed on tiny plants and animals, called **plankton**, which float in the water.

Polar bears can run faster than humans.

11

The smallest living things in the sea are called plankton. They are so small that you could fit 40,000 of them on the end of your thumb.

Plankton can be either plants or animals. They are food for the larger sea animals.

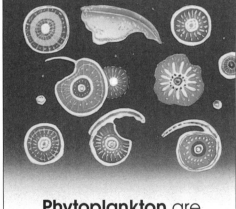

Large clouds of plankton drift in the surface waters of all seas.

Phytoplankton are microscopic plants. They use the sunlight's energy to grow like plants on land.

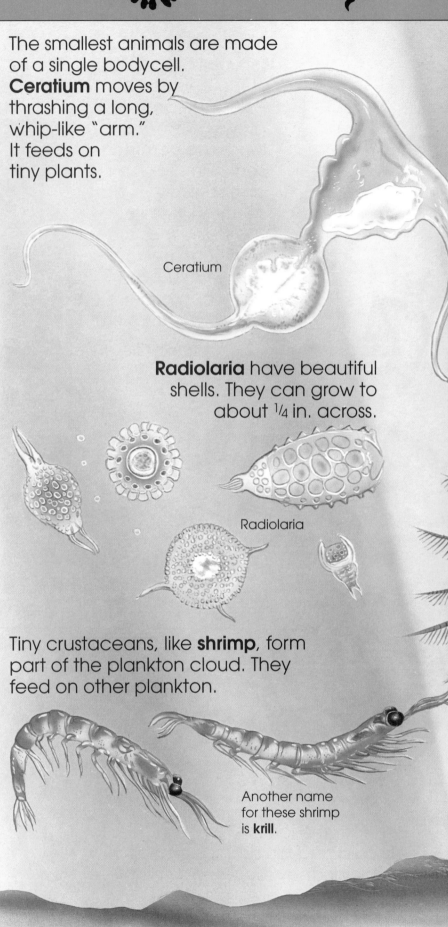

The smallest animals are made of a single bodycell. **Ceratium** moves by thrashing a long, whip-like "arm." It feeds on tiny plants.

Ceratium

Radiolaria have beautiful shells. They can grow to about ¼ in. across.

Radiolaria

Tiny crustaceans, like **shrimp**, form part of the plankton cloud. They feed on other plankton.

Another name for these shrimp is **krill**.

Some of the **plankton** are the young of much larger creatures. Because they drift with the ocean currents, these creatures can travel much further than they can as adults, allowing them to reach new homes.

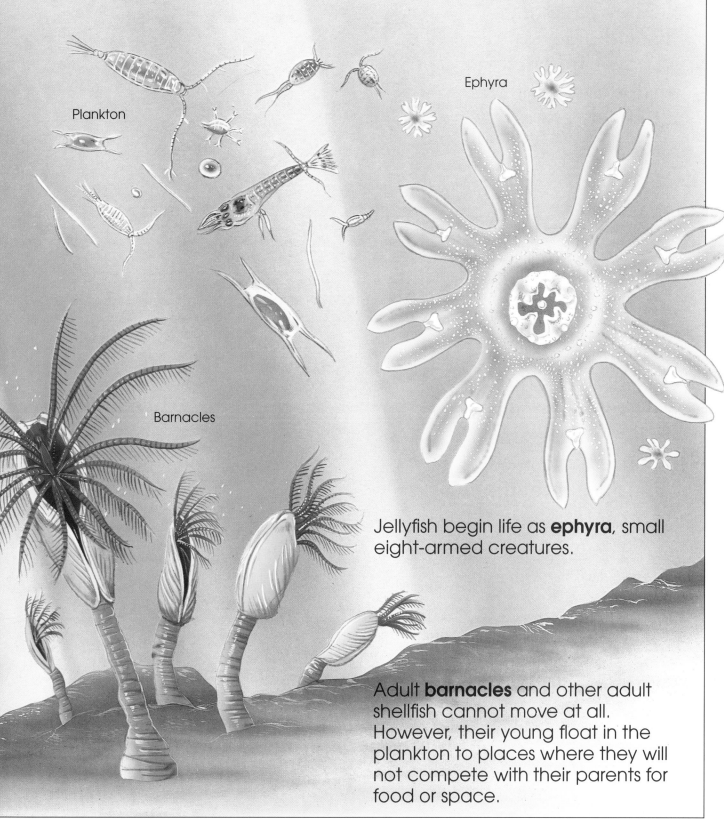

Ephyra

Plankton

Barnacles

Jellyfish begin life as **ephyra**, small eight-armed creatures.

Adult **barnacles** and other adult shellfish cannot move at all. However, their young float in the plankton to places where they will not compete with their parents for food or space.

Whales are mammals which have evolved to live in the sea. They have fins instead of legs and a powerful tail to push them through the water.

Like all mammals, whales breathe air, so they need to come to the surface from time to time.

The **bowhead whale's** head is 20 ft. long. This is one-third of its length. The jaws are packed with baleen to filter food from the seawater.

The largest whales feed on plankton. They have special filters, called baleen, in their mouths which strain seawater and remove the tiny animals and plants to be eaten.

The earliest known whale is **basiliosaurus**, which lived about 40 million years ago.

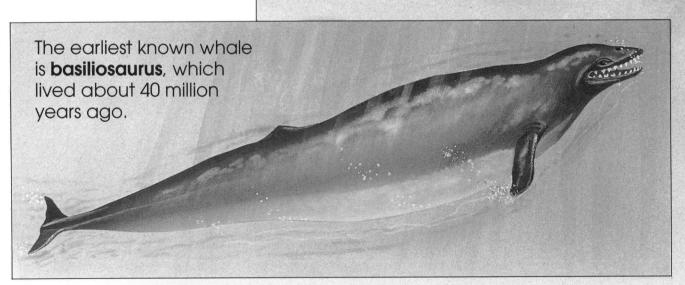

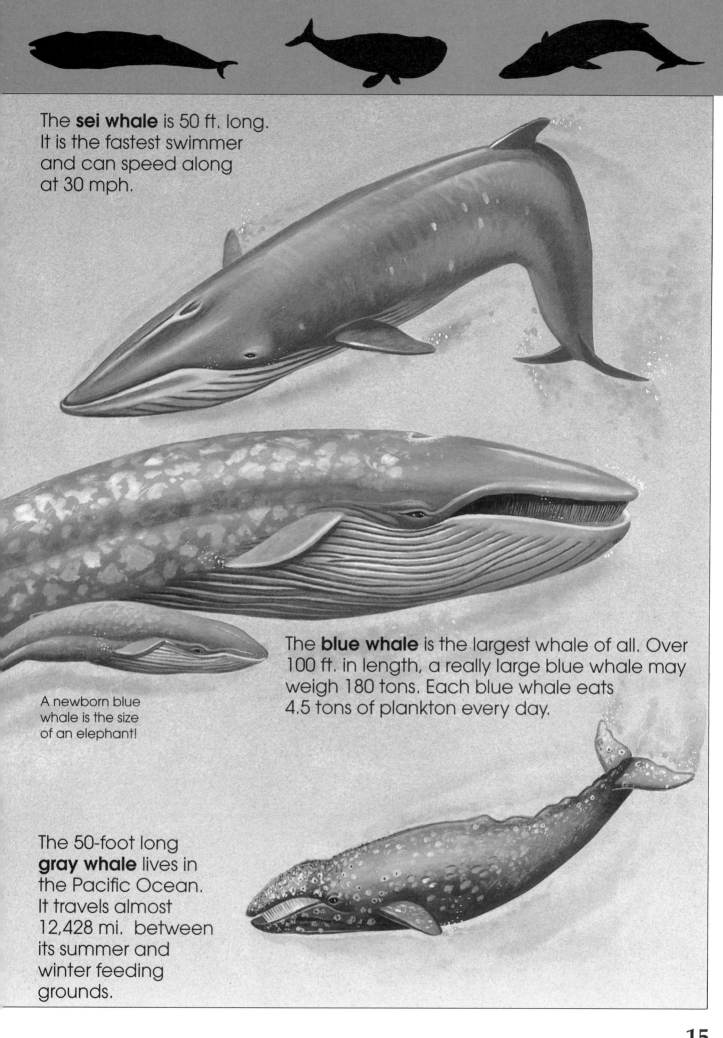

The **sei whale** is 50 ft. long. It is the fastest swimmer and can speed along at 30 mph.

The **blue whale** is the largest whale of all. Over 100 ft. in length, a really large blue whale may weigh 180 tons. Each blue whale eats 4.5 tons of plankton every day.

A newborn blue whale is the size of an elephant!

The 50-foot long **gray whale** lives in the Pacific Ocean. It travels almost 12,428 mi. between its summer and winter feeding grounds.

15

Coastline creatures

Seals are mammals which have evolved to live in the oceans.

Their legs have become flippers to help them swim, but they can still move on land.

Seals spend some of their time on shore, either caring for their babies or resting from hunting for fish.

Elephant seals were once hunted for the rich oil their bodies contain. At one time, only about a hundred were still alive, but today there are over 50,000 of them.

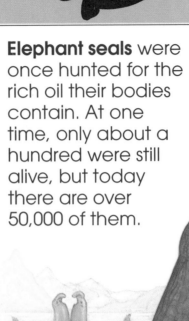

The **harp seal** hunts fish beneath the ocean surface. Thick layers of fat under its skin protect it from the icy water.

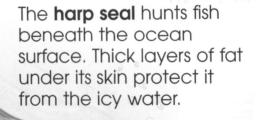

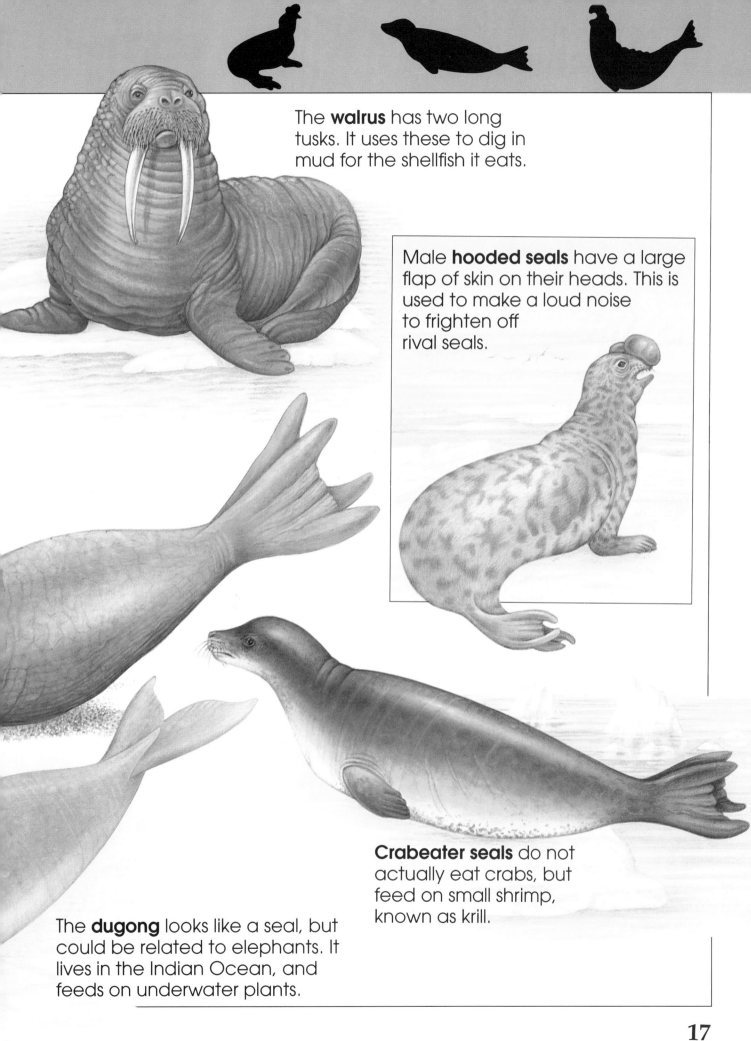

The **walrus** has two long tusks. It uses these to dig in mud for the shellfish it eats.

Male **hooded seals** have a large flap of skin on their heads. This is used to make a loud noise to frighten off rival seals.

Crabeater seals do not actually eat crabs, but feed on small shrimp, known as krill.

The **dugong** looks like a seal, but could be related to elephants. It lives in the Indian Ocean, and feeds on underwater plants.

Dolphins belong to a group of whales called toothed whales. They do not eat plankton but hunt squid and fish.

Dolphins are very intelligent creatures. They communicate with each other using different sounds arranged like words in a sentence.

Some dolphins are very rare. The **shepherd's beaked whale** is a recent discovery.

Dolphins are social animals. They live in family groups. If one dolphin is sick or injured, others will come to its rescue.

Dolphins are mammals. They breathe air and feed their babies with milk.

The **bouto** is a dolphin that lives in the Amazon River.

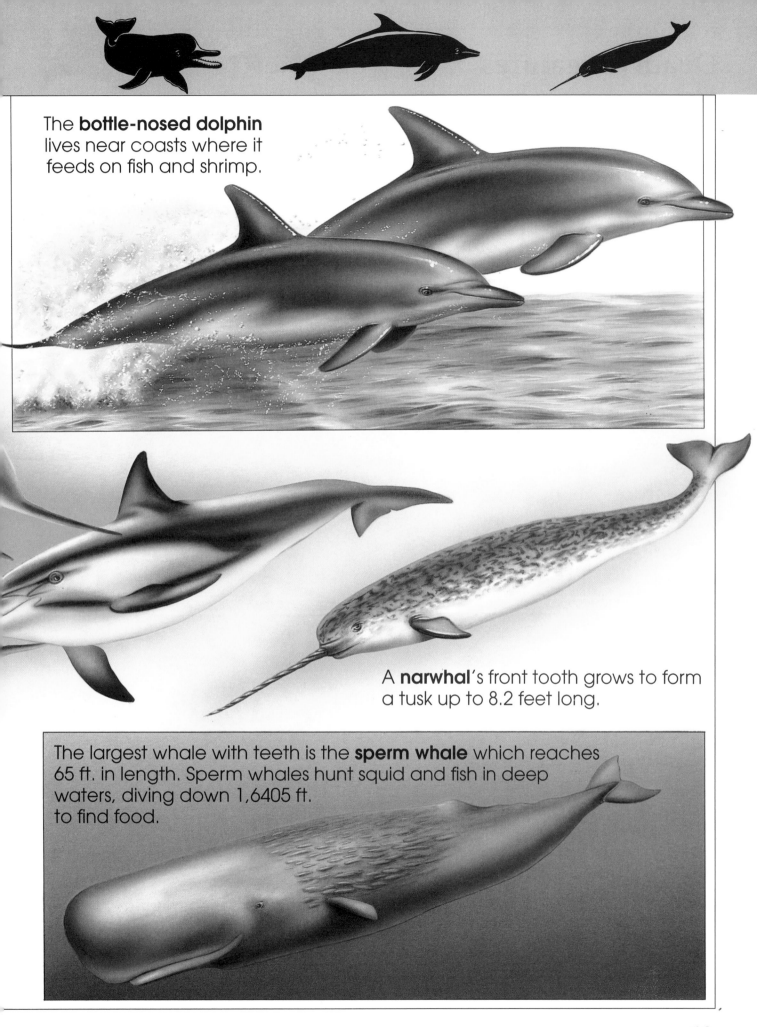

The **bottle-nosed dolphin** lives near coasts where it feeds on fish and shrimp.

A **narwhal**'s front tooth grows to form a tusk up to 8.2 feet long.

The largest whale with teeth is the **sperm whale** which reaches 65 ft. in length. Sperm whales hunt squid and fish in deep waters, diving down 1,6405 ft. to find food.

Sharks and rays are found in all seas. Their skeletons are made of soft cartilage instead of hard bone.

Sharks hunt other sea creatures, using their sharp teeth and strong muscles to overpower their prey.

The largest shark is the 60-foot long **whale shark**. Unlike most sharks, it does not hunt other animals. Instead, it feeds on plankton.

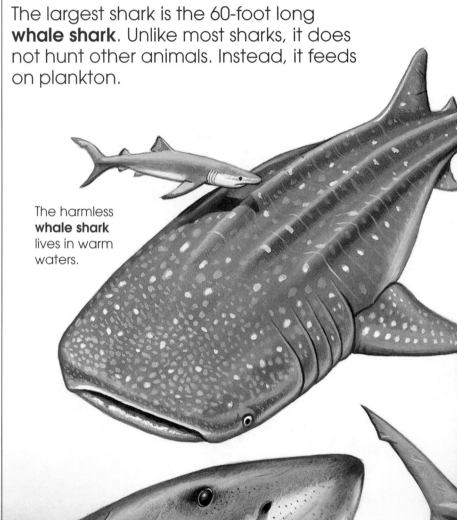

The harmless **whale shark** lives in warm waters.

The **great white shark** sometimes attacks people.

The largest hunting shark is the **great white shark**. It may grow to 23 ft. long and usually feeds on larger fish and other animals.

Receptors on the head of the **hammerhead** shark help it to detect its prey. It swings its head from side to side as it swims.

The **manta** is a giant ray. Its wings can measure 23 feet across. Sometimes it jumps out of the sea, creating a large splash when it falls back.

The **thresher shark** uses its long tail to beat the water when hunting. Experts think that this may stun fish, making them easy to catch.

The **stingray** has a large, poisonous spine on top of its tail, which it uses to fight off attackers.

Large groups, called mobs, of **blue sharks** are often found in tropical oceans. As many as a thousand blue sharks may form one mob.

21

Flying creatures

Many birds live at sea feeding on fish or other sea creatures.

Most sea birds nest on islands, where their eggs and young are safe from attack.

Sea birds often make long journeys between their nesting sites and feeding grounds. Arctic terns travel between the Arctic and the Antarctic.

The **great skua** is a large bird, over 20 in. long. It hunts other sea birds, as well as fish.

Herring gulls are very common. They feed on fish and shrimp, but will also fly inland to raid garbage dumps and picnic areas.

A **skimmer** finds fish by flying just above the surface of the sea, with its bill in the water. As soon as the bill strikes a fish, it is snapped up.

The largest sea bird is the **wandering albatross**, which has wings 11 feet across. Long ago, sailors believed it was bad luck to kill an albatross.

Steamer ducks live around the coast. They cannot fly, but swim along the shore looking for shellfish, shrimp and crabs to eat.

Puffins nest on cliffs and rocky islands. The females lay just one egg each year.

Gannet fly around searching for fish in the water. They may dive from a height of 100 ft. to catch their prey.

23

Reptiles are animals such as lizards. Most live on land.

A few types of reptile have evolved to live in the ocean, but they need to come to the surface often to breathe air.

Most sea reptiles lay their eggs on dry land. They may come ashore once a year to do this.

The **green turtle** has a tough shell to protect it from attack. It feeds on seaweed and jellyfish.

The **leatherback turtle** has no shell, but the skin on its back is very thick and tough.

Estuary crocodiles live off the coasts of northern Australia. They can grow to be over 20 ft. long and are the largest sea reptiles alive today.

Ridley turtles crunch up shellfish with their strong jaws.

The **banded sea snake** lives in the Pacific Ocean where it hunts fish. It is one of the most poisonous snakes in the world.

The **hawksbill turtle** is very rare. Not long ago, it was hunted for its shell. This was used to make things such as ornate boxes and spectacle frames.

Marine iguanas live around the remote Galapagos Islands in the Pacific Ocean. They dive into the ocean to feed on seaweed.

Marine iguanas come ashore to bask in the sun.

Strange creatures

There are many fish in the oceans that look strange to us, but they are actually very well adapted to their surroundings.

Thousands of fish have evolved to live in different places - on coral reefs, in icy waters, near the surface of the sea, or on the seabed

Flying fish are able to leap out of the water and glide through the air, using their fins as wings. It is thought that the fish "fly" in this way to escape hunters.

When danger threatens, the **porcupine fish** gulps huge amounts of water and swells up to four times its usual size. The stiff spines stick out to make the fish look like a spiky football.

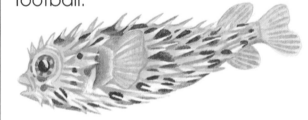

The **four-eyed fish** swims at the surface with each of its two eyes half in and half out of the water. The fish looks for insect prey on the surface, while watching for danger under the sea.

The **swordfish** has a bony upper jaw which can be over 1 yard long and shaped like a sword. Nobody knows what the sword is used for.

The **sailfish** is the fastest fish in the sea. It can reach speeds of 68 mph.

The **coelacanth** lives in the deep waters of the Indian Ocean. Before it was caught in 1938, the coelacanth was known only from fossils dating back 60 million years. Scientists thought it had been extinct ever since.

Porcupine fish

The **sea dragon** is only 16 in. long. It swims near seaweed where it can hide easily.

Prehistoric creatures

Millions of years ago, strange creatures lived in the oceans.

Scientists know about these creatures because they have found fossils of their bones buried in ancient rocks.

Many of these giant sea animals lived at the same time as the dinosaurs.

Kronosaurus had the largest head of any hunter in the sea. It was almost 10 ft. long and was armed with lots of sharp teeth.

Cryptocleidus had strong flippers to propel it through the water. It caught small fish in its long jaws armed with sharp teeth.

Archelon was the largest turtle. It was nearly 13 feet long and lived about 70 million years ago.

Ichthyosaurus looked like a dolphin or large fish, but was really a reptile. Ichthyosaurus could not come on shore to lay eggs like most reptiles, so it gave birth to live young.

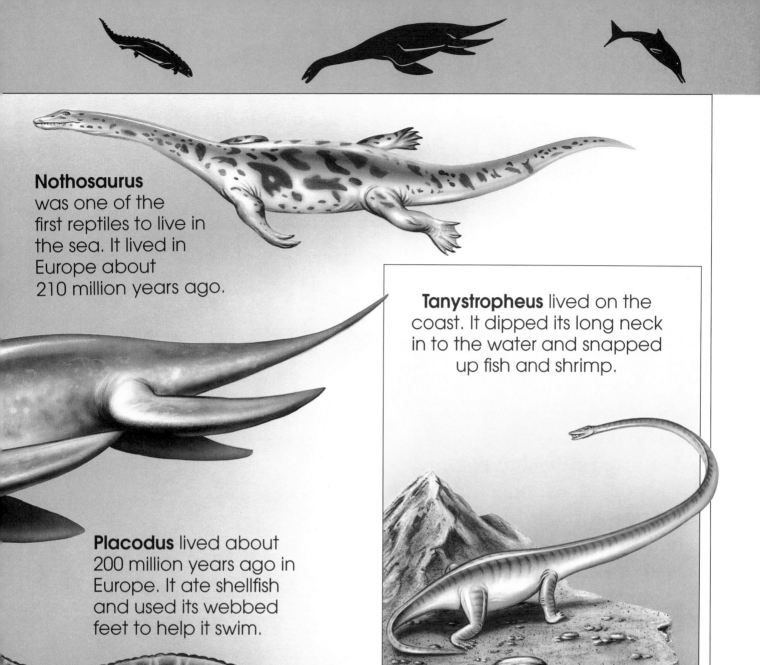

Nothosaurus was one of the first reptiles to live in the sea. It lived in Europe about 210 million years ago.

Tanystropheus lived on the coast. It dipped its long neck in to the water and snapped up fish and shrimp.

Placodus lived about 200 million years ago in Europe. It ate shellfish and used its webbed feet to help it swim.

Placodus

Metrioryhnchus

Metriorhynchus was a 10-foot long crocodile which lived in the ocean 140 million years ago. It was so adapted to life in the sea that it even had a fish-like tail.

Because the oceans are so vast, there are many areas which have never been explored properly.

Sailors who have traveled off the main shipping routes have reported seeing strange and curious creatures. As nobody has ever caught one of these mysterious creatures, scientists do not believe they really exist.

The type of **sea monster** most often seen has a small head and a long neck held upright. Witnesses say they see a large body under the water with four large fins which move the creature slowly along.

This sea monster looks like a prehistoric sea animal, **elamosaurus**, which was about 33 feet long.

The 13-foot long **megamouth shark** was not discovered until the 1980s. Nobody knew about it until one was accidentally caught in a net. This proved that large sea creatures can exist without anybody knowing about them.

Manatees swim slowly in shallow coastal waters, feeding on water plants.

Long ago, sailors believed in **mermaids**. Today, scientists know that what they probably saw were seal-like creatures called **manatees**.

The **sea serpent** is supposed to be a gigantic, snake-like creature up to 100 feet long. Many people have reported seeing them.

A giant turtle-like creature was seen in 1877 by the crew of *HMS Osborne*. The creature was about 65 feet long and swam quickly.

Young **scorpions** are carried on their mother's back.

Many young minibeasts look like small versions of their parents. They simply grow into adults. Others look completely different. They develop into adults through stages.

Some young minibeasts that look like small adults, such as snails, grow very gradually. Others, such as insects, have a hard outer skeleton. They have to molt in order to grow.

They molt by making a new, soft skeleton beneath the hard one. The new skeleton is pumped up with air, and this splits the old skeleton. The young minibeast grows inside the new, hard skeleton.

Cockroaches lay their eggs in a hard purse-shaped case. When the young hatch, they look like small adults.

Cockroaches can produce 30,000 young in a single year!

Young **snails** look like miniature adults when they hatch from round, silvery-colored eggs. As they grow, more coils are added to their shells.

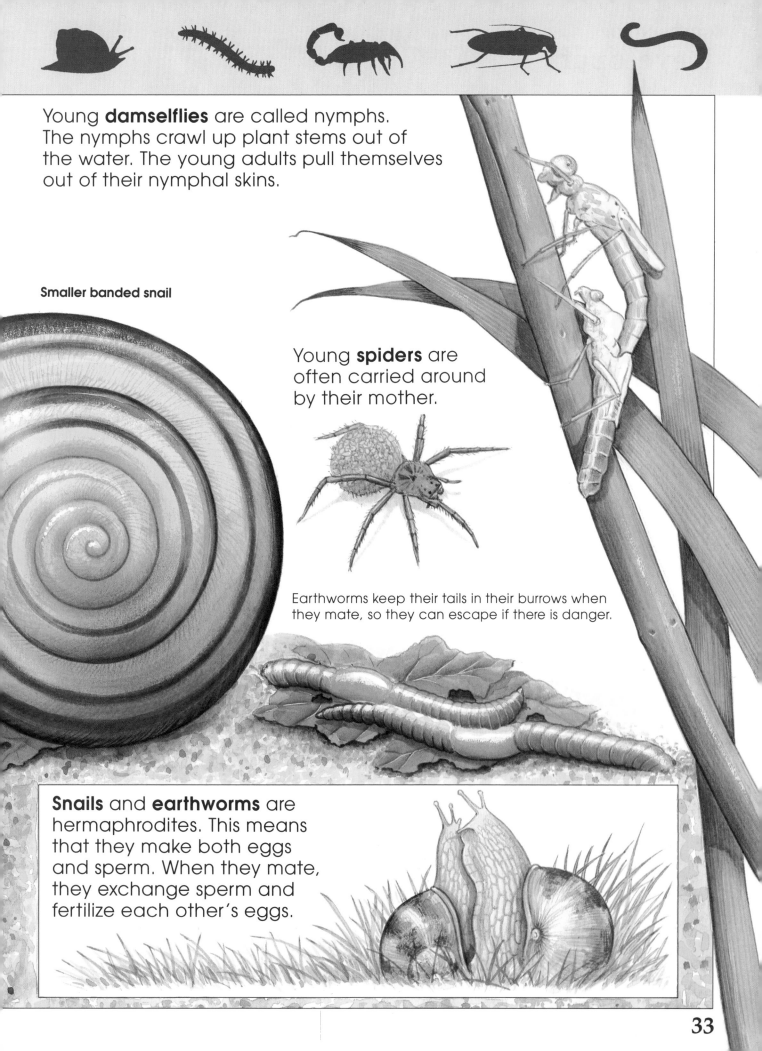

Young **damselflies** are called nymphs. The nymphs crawl up plant stems out of the water. The young adults pull themselves out of their nymphal skins.

Smaller banded snail

Young **spiders** are often carried around by their mother.

Earthworms keep their tails in their burrows when they mate, so they can escape if there is danger.

Snails and **earthworms** are hermaphrodites. This means that they make both eggs and sperm. When they mate, they exchange sperm and fertilize each other's eggs.

When they are born, many young minibeasts look completely different from their parents. They go through several stages to develop into adults.

The young that hatch from the eggs are called larvae. A larva feeds and grows. It eventually develops into a chrysalis, which is also called a pupa. Inside the chrysalis, the larva changes into an adult. After a time, the adult emerges from the chrysalis.

The development of a larva into an adult through these stages is called metamorphosis.

Lady bug beetles and their larvae feed on aphids.

Caddis fly larvae live underwater. They make homes to live in by sticking together pieces of plant, sand, shells and other material. They carry their homes around with them.

The larvae of **butterflies** and **moths** develop into adults through metamorphosis.

This egg has been laid by a **pasha** butterfly.

This **pasha** caterpillar will turn into a chrysalis.

A caddis fly larva develops into a chrysalis in its home. It then leaves its home and swims to the water surface to become an adult.

You can watch young caterpillars grow by keeping them in a jar with some food. You should ask an adult to make a hole in the lid of the jar. Cover the jar with greaseproof paper with tiny holes in it, and replace the lid. This will allow the caterpillars to breathe.

Black fly larvae live in streams and ponds. They attach themselves to rocks with the sucker on their rear.

Adult black flies suck blood. Some of them carry diseases which they inject when they suck the blood.

Inside the chrysalis, the **pasha** caterpillar changes.

The adult **pasha** butterfly emerges from the chrysalis.

Hunters and trappers

Minibeasts have to find food to eat in order to grow. Some of them eat the leaves, shoots, flowers, fruits and roots of plants. Many minibeasts even eat other minibeasts!

Minibeasts find their food in different ways. Some of them eat rotten plants or animals, while others suck juices from plants, or even blood from animals!

Some minibeasts tunnel and burrow through the soil, while others hunt for a meal on the surface of the ground. Some minibeasts even make traps in which they catch their prey.

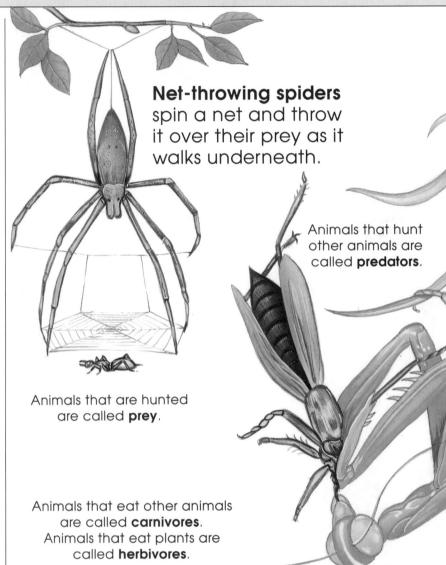

Net-throwing spiders spin a net and throw it over their prey as it walks underneath.

Animals that hunt other animals are called **predators**.

Animals that are hunted are called **prey**.

Animals that eat other animals are called **carnivores**. Animals that eat plants are called **herbivores**.

Long-jawed spiders are well camouflaged on grass as they wait for their prey to walk past.

Trap-door spiders hide in a silk-lined burrow with a trap door at the entrance. They throw open the trap door to grasp their prey.

Praying mantids are very well camouflaged. They seize their prey with their spiney forelegs and feed on it upside-down.

Antlion larvae lie half-hidden at the bottom of a funnel-shaped pit. They flick sand at minibeasts that slip over the edge of the pit, so that the minibeasts fall down to the bottom.

Blue-black spider wasps have a loud buzz which terrifies their prey.

Euglandina rosea attacking a *papustyla* snail.

Tiger beetles are fierce hunters. They use their strong jaws to kill and cut up their prey, which includes young lizards.

Snails sometimes attack and eat other snails. If the snail has withdrawn inside its shell, the attacker will drill a hole through the shell to eat the snail.

Suckers

Some minibeasts live on liquid food. They have extremely sharp mouthparts which they use to pierce the skin of an animal or the tissue of a plant.

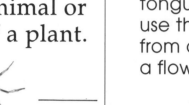

They usually suck blood or plant juices through a sucking tube.

Oleander Hawkmoths hover in the air like hummingbirds. Their tongues are 4.8 in. long. They use them to suck nectar from deep within a flower.

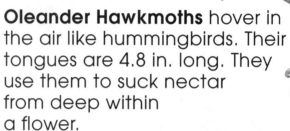

Fleas use the hooks and spines on their bodies to hold tightly on to the fur or skin of their hosts. Fleas can carry diseases which they inject into their hosts when they bite.

In the Middle Ages, the disease called the Black Death was spread by the rat flea. This disease killed millions of people.

Ticks are parasites. They sink their hooked mouthparts into the flesh of their host. As they suck the blood, their round, elastic bodies swell greatly.

Aphids feed on plant juices. Their delicate mouthparts pierce the sap vessels inside a plant, and the pressure forces sweet-tasting sap into the aphid's body.

Some of the sap is passed out of the aphid as a drop of sweet fluid. This is sometimes eaten by ants.

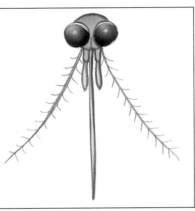

The long, needle-sharp mouthparts of a mosquito contain a sucking tube.

Mosquitoes feed on blood and plant juices. Female mosquitoes have a meal of blood before they lay their eggs. Male mosquitoes suck plant juices instead of blood.

Female mosquitoes bite humans. A person can lose over a pint of blood in an hour.

Jungle leeches suck blood. When they have had a blood meal, their body swells.

Animals that live and feed on other animals are called **parasites**. The animals that provide a home and food are called **hosts**.

Thrips are tiny "thunder-bugs." They have mouthpieces on one side of their mouth only, which they use to suck plant juices.

Thrips are pests, feeding on corn and other crops.

Robber flies catch and stab their prey with their sharp mouthpieces. Their victim is then sucked dry.

Cochineal bugs suck plant juices. They are used to make food coloring as they are dark red.

Minibeasts have to get around in order to find food, a mate and a new place to live. They also need to be able to escape from predators.

Minibeasts use many ways of getting around. Some of them crawl and others run. Some of them jump and others wriggle. Some of them can even fly.

Most minibeasts that fly have two pairs of wings which beat together.

Spiders are minibeasts that can fly but do not have wings!

A young **wolf spider** has released a long, silken thread. The wind will pluck the thread into the air, whisking the young spider away with it.

Beetles have two pairs of wings. The first pair is very tough and protects the delicate flying wings which are folded underneath when not in use.

Dragonflies chase other flying minibeasts by rapidly beating their outstretched wings.

Emperor dragonfly

Damselflies fly by fluttering their wings. They catch other flying minibeasts by grasping them with their legs.

40

Butterflies fly during the daytime. Most of them slowly flap their large, colorful wings.

Flies are the best acrobats of the minibeast world. They can even land upside-down on a ceiling.

The wings of the **painted lady** warn other minibeasts to keep away.

Flies have only one pair of real wings. The rear wings are tiny bat-shaped objects which beat very fast.

The wings of the **swallowtail** make a noise as they clap together.

Hover flies can hover, dart backward and forward, and even fly straight upward.

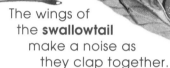

Midges have one of the fastest wing beats. Some beat their wings over 1,000 times a second.

Fairy flies have delicate, feathery wings. They are one of the smallest flying minibeasts.

Cockchafers fly at dusk. They can fly over 3 miles in search of a mate.

Crawlers and runners

Many minibeasts get around by crawling or running. Some of them have lots of short legs which they use to crawl about.

Other minibeasts have fewer legs, but they are usually quite long. Long legs allow the minibeast to run about quickly.

Pseudoscorpions can run backward as well as forward! They are active hunters that crawl among decaying leaves in search of a meal.

Pseudoscorpions have long sensitive hairs on their rear to help them feel where they are going.

Caterpillars usually have plenty of food around them. As they do not need to move far to find a meal, they have short legs.

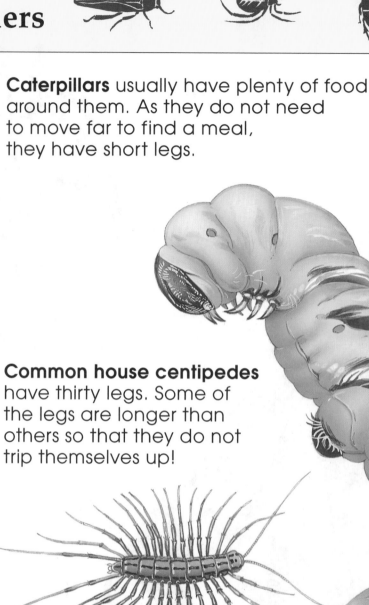

Common house centipedes have thirty legs. Some of the legs are longer than others so that they do not trip themselves up!

Harvest spiders have very long legs and a small body. To prevent them from toppling over, they bend their legs and keep their body close to the ground.

The legs of harvest spiders are not used for speed. The spiders crawl through the vegetation where they live.

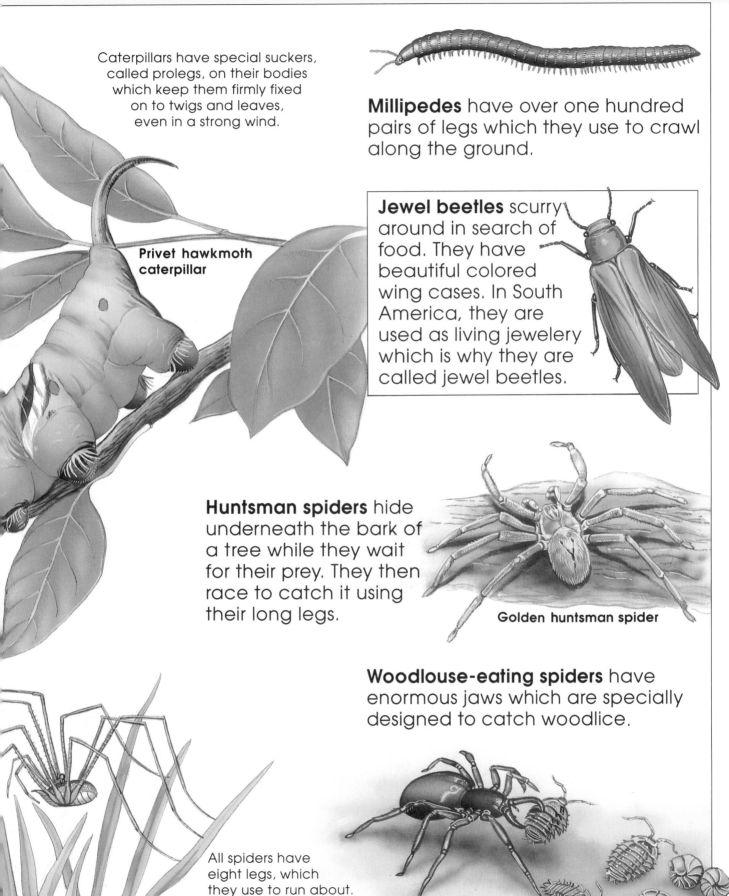

Caterpillars have special suckers, called prolegs, on their bodies which keep them firmly fixed on to twigs and leaves, even in a strong wind.

Millipedes have over one hundred pairs of legs which they use to crawl along the ground.

Privet hawkmoth caterpillar

Jewel beetles scurry around in search of food. They have beautiful colored wing cases. In South America, they are used as living jewelery which is why they are called jewel beetles.

Huntsman spiders hide underneath the bark of a tree while they wait for their prey. They then race to catch it using their long legs.

Golden huntsman spider

Woodlouse-eating spiders have enormous jaws which are specially designed to catch woodlice.

All spiders have eight legs, which they use to run about.

43

Hoppers, jumpers and skaters

Some minibeasts move around by hopping and jumping. Being able to jump suddenly is a good way to catch a meal, or to escape from a predator.

Other minibeasts skate across the surface of water in search of food or a mate.

Raft spiders stand half on the water and half on a water plant. They race across the water surface to catch their prey, which includes small fish.

Grasshoppers and **crickets** have huge back legs. They use the strong muscles in these legs to catapult themselves high into the air.

Fleas have large back legs which allow them to jump very high - well over half a yard.

Fleas jump onto animals, such as cats, where they make their home.

Treehoppers hop from tree to tree in search of food.

Pond skaters have waterproof hairs on their feet which help them to float on the water surface.

Grasshoppers attract a mate by rubbing their back legs against their front wings to make a singing sound.

Springtails can spring suddenly into the air using their special "tail."

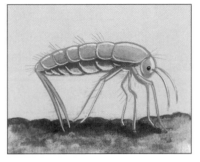

The "tail" is tucked under the springtail's body.

The "tail" straightens suddenly, making the springtail spring into the air.

Jumping plant lice have very strong back legs which means they can jump from plant to plant.

Click beetles have a peg on their bodies. When they lie on their backs and bend, the peg pops free with a loud click, and they jump into the air.

Apple suckers are jumping plant lice which live on apple trees.

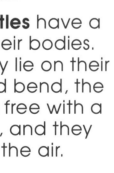

Whirligig beetles skate quickly across the surface of a pond in a zigzag pattern.

Jumping spiders have excellent sight. When they see a fly, they will leap into the air to catch it.

Slitherers and wrigglers

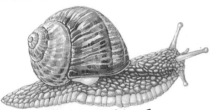

Legs can get in the way, so some minibeasts do not have any legs at all. They have soft bodies, and they move around by slithering along the ground or wriggling through the soil.

Earthworms make burrows which let air into the soil. They drag leaves into the burrows for food.

Leeches move along by using their suckers. They have two suckers on their bodies, one at the front and one at the rear. The one at the front has teeth as it is also their mouth.

The rear sucker sticks to the ground and the body stretches forward.

The front sucker sticks to the ground and the body is pulled forward.

African giant snail

Earthworms burrow through the soil by eating it. They grip the soil with very small bristles along their bodies.

You can make a wormery by putting some earthworms and compost into a plastic bucket with small holes in the bottom. As the earthworms eat the compost, you will need to add some more to the bucket.

Slugs and snails are special minibeasts that slither along on a trail of slime using one foot. If you place a slug or snail on a piece of clear plastic and look at it from underneath, you will see ripples moving along the foot as the minibeast moves forward.

Hover fly larvae look like little leeches. They wriggle along in search of aphids which they eat.

Fly larvae hatch from eggs laid on dung. They have small legs, or no legs at all. To move about, they wriggle through their squidgy food.

Soil centipedes have up to 100 pairs of tiny legs which help them to grip the soil.

Nematodes are minute roundworms which live inside many animals and plants, and in soil. They move around by wriggling their tiny bodies.

Some minibeasts hide from predators or prey, while others display bright colors, make noises, or glow at night to attract attention.

Many minibeasts use colors and shapes to disguise themselves. Some blend into their background, which is called camouflage. Others pretend to be fierce minibeasts.

Some minibeasts use bright colors to frighten or warn their predators. Others use sound and light to "talk" to each other and attract a mate.

Assassin bug larvae look like the surrounding soil.

Peppered moths blend into the bark of the tree trunk on which they are resting.

Some peppered moths are darker. They hide on tree trunks which have been blackened by pollution.

African bush-crickets are perfectly camouflaged among the leaves.

Stick insects are well hidden from predators as they look like the twigs they are sitting on.

Stick insects can be kept in a large jar as pets.

Banded snails have different shells.

The snails with pale shells live in dry, pale green grass.

The snails with dark shells live in lush green vegetation.

Flower mantids are well camouflaged as they lie in wait for their prey.

Brimstone butterflies look like the green ivy leaves that they rest on.

Crab spiders are predators that hide within flowers, waiting to pounce on visiting insects.

49

Tricksters

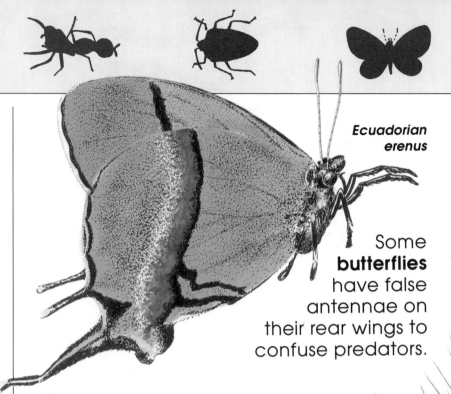

Ecuadorian erenus

Many minibeasts try to trick predators by using different disguises. Some of them have the same colors as minibeasts that are fierce or poisonous, so that predators will leave them alone.

Some **butterflies** have false antennae on their rear wings to confuse predators.

Tussock moth caterpillars have fine irritating hairs on their body which give predators a nasty shock!

Other minibeasts let predators approach them, but then they give them a nasty surprise. A few minibeasts even use false heads to confuse their predators!

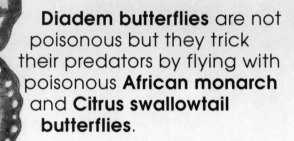

Diadem butterflies are not poisonous but they trick their predators by flying with poisonous **African monarch** and **Citrus swallowtail butterflies**.

Citrus
swallowtail

African
monarch

Wasp beetles are not dangerous as they do not sting. They pretend to be wasps to trick their predators.

Copying the color of another creature is called **mimicry**. This helps to protect harmless minibeasts from predators.

Some **jumping spiders** mimic mutillid wasps to protect themselves.

The jumping spider's rear looks like the head of a mutillid wasp.

Shieldbugs ooze a stinking liquid when they are in danger. This is why they are also called stinkbugs.

Golden-silk spiders have bright colors. At a distance, these break up the shape of the spider, making it difficult to see.

Diadem

Flashers and warners

Many minibeasts use bright colors to protect themselves. Some of them frighten their predators by suddenly flashing bright colors at them.

Some minibeasts show their bright colors all the time. Predators learn that these are warning colors, telling them that the minibeast is dangerous.

There are only a few warning colors: black, white, yellow, red and brown. Minibeasts learn quickly that these colors warn of danger.

Peacock butterflies have large colorful eye spots on their wings.

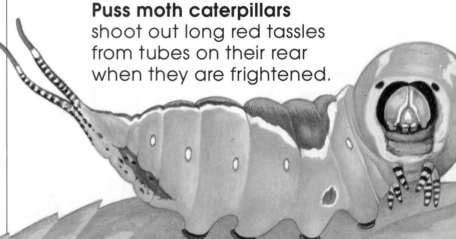

Puss moth caterpillars shoot out long red tassles from tubes on their rear when they are frightened.

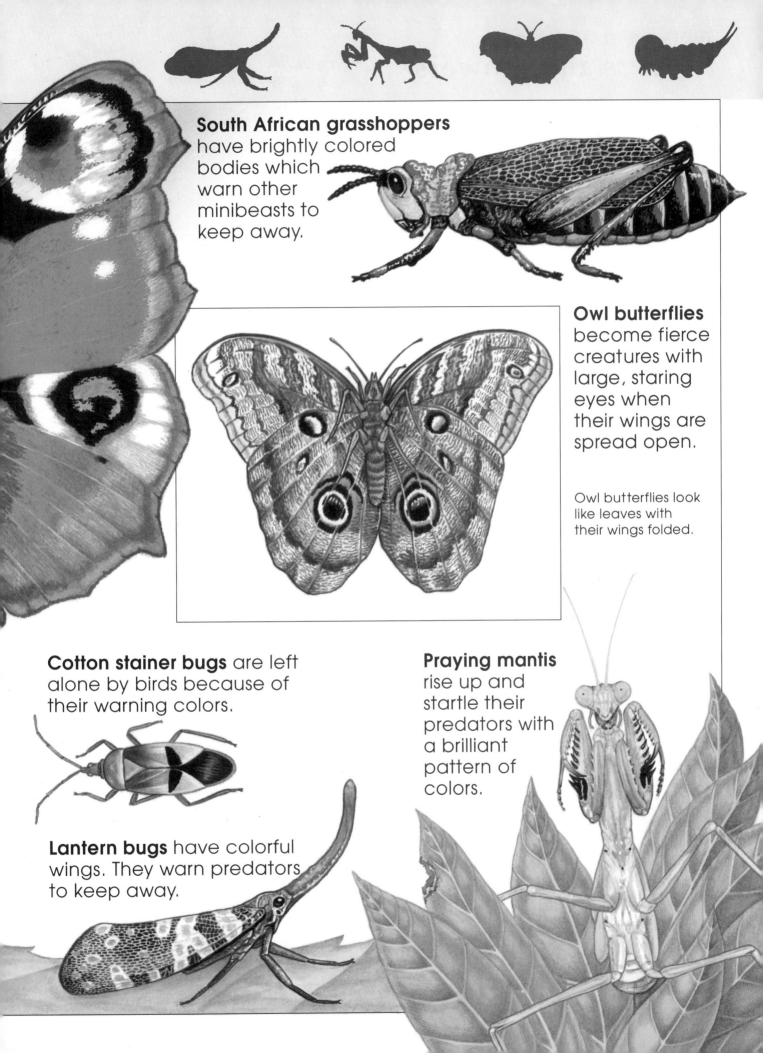

South African grasshoppers have brightly colored bodies which warn other minibeasts to keep away.

Owl butterflies become fierce creatures with large, staring eyes when their wings are spread open.

Owl butterflies look like leaves with their wings folded.

Cotton stainer bugs are left alone by birds because of their warning colors.

Praying mantis rise up and startle their predators with a brilliant pattern of colors.

Lantern bugs have colorful wings. They warn predators to keep away.

Many minibeasts use sound to attract a mate, or to warn off predators. Some of them make sounds during the day. If you walk through a field or a forest, you may hear all kinds of chirps and buzzes.

Many minibeasts make sounds at night, while others use light to attract a mate. The males or females glow in the dark, and their mates are attracted to them.

Katydids sing their repetitive song "katydid, katydidn't" at night. They sing by rubbing their left front wing against a ridge on the right wing.

Katydids and other crickets have ears on their legs.

Tree crickets make thousands of piercing chirps without stopping. Some tree crickets can be heard 1 mi. away!

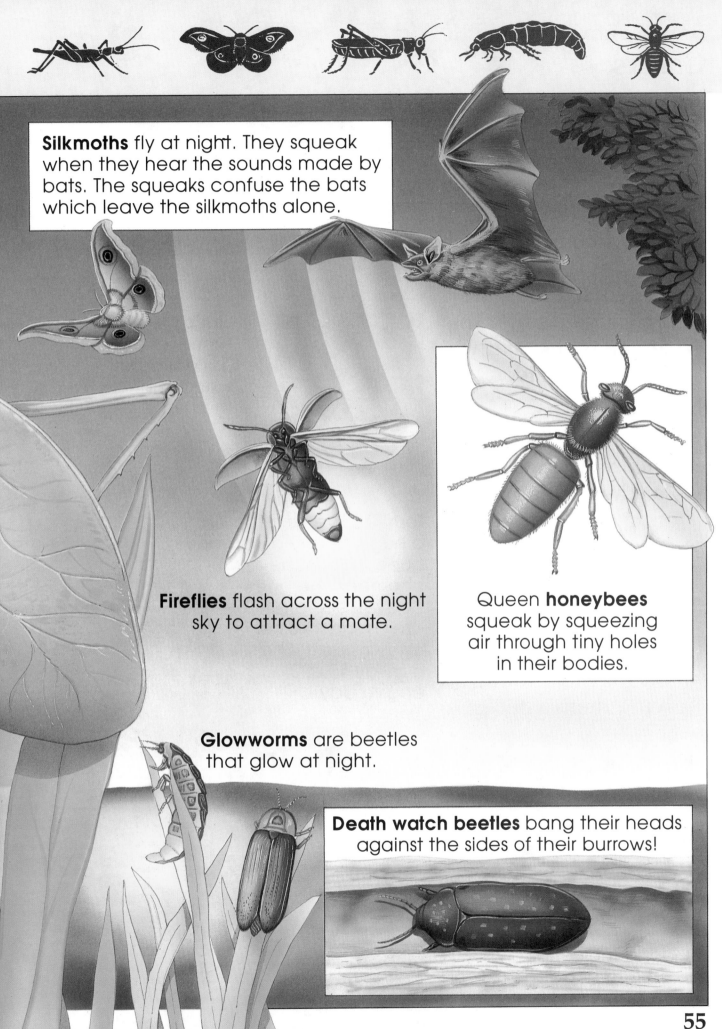

Silkmoths fly at night. They squeak when they hear the sounds made by bats. The squeaks confuse the bats which leave the silkmoths alone.

Fireflies flash across the night sky to attract a mate.

Queen **honeybees** squeak by squeezing air through tiny holes in their bodies.

Glowworms are beetles that glow at night.

Death watch beetles bang their heads against the sides of their burrows!

Most minibeasts leave their young to look after themselves. Many of the young starve to death, or are eaten by predators. To overcome this, many eggs are laid.

Some minibeasts care for their eggs and young, so fewer eggs need to be laid. Minibeasts such as female ants or bees work together to provide shelter and food for their young, giving them a better chance of survival.

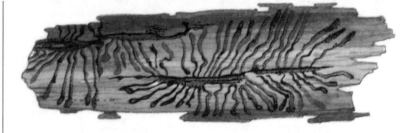

Look at the bark of fallen trees and see if you can find the tunnels of bark beetles.

Elm bark beetles tunnel under the bark of a tree where they lay their eggs.

Termites live as a family in a huge nest. The king and queen live in the royal chamber. The queen's body swells to a huge size as she lays her eggs inside it. She can lay 30,000 eggs a day.

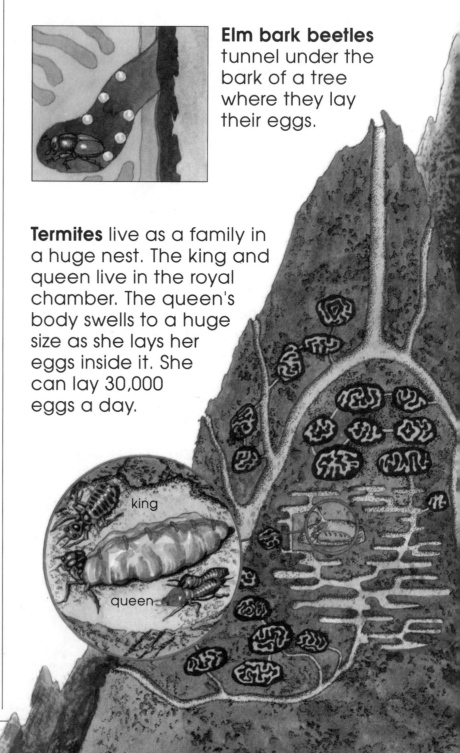

king

queen

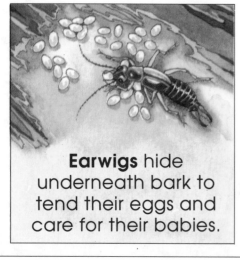

Earwigs hide underneath bark to tend their eggs and care for their babies.

Tailor ants make nests out of leaves. The workers sew the leaves together with silk made by the saliva glands of the larvae!

Pseudoscorpions carry their eggs on their bodies and feed them "milk." They look after their eggs and young inside a tiny nest made of silk.

Queen **bumblebees** build a wax honeypot in the nest where they lay their eggs, so they have plenty of food. They care for the young on their own.

Sandwasps catch and sting a caterpillar. This sends it to sleep. They put it in a burrow in the sand, and lay an egg on it.

When the egg hatches, the larva feeds on the sleeping caterpillar.

Oak gall wasps lay their eggs on the rib of an oak leaf. The rib swells and forms a gall which is a safe home for the larvae that grow inside it.

Galls come in all shapes and sizes. The aleppo gall is used to make special permanent ink which is used by banks.

Pythons swallow their prey whole.

Giant **pythons** coil their powerful bodies around their helpless prey until they suffocate it.

Happily there are few really monstrous large animals. Smaller monsters are much more common.

The **elephant** is the largest land mammal. A full grown male (bull) African elephant can be over 10 ft. tall and weigh 9 tons.

Many large animals might look frightening, but usually they do not attack unless they are threatened.

The enormous **Komodo Dragon** prowls through the forest on lonely Indonesian islands.

This fierce lizard, nearly three meters long, will even attack people.

A **tiger** has huge, sharp teeth which grip and kill its prey.

The **giraffe** is the tallest mammal on Earth. However, it is not fierce and eats only leaves.

Grizzly bears tower a frightening 10 ft. when they stand upright on their hind legs. They have big, sharp claws for tearing at food.

Gorillas are the largest primates. When threatened, a male gorilla will beat his chest with his hands, roar and rush toward the enemy.

The **Goliath beetle** is a heavy weight champion of the insect world. It can carry a load 850 times its own weight. That is similar to a human carrying 67 tons.

Some of the strangest monsters can be found swimming and living in the sea.

Large ones like the whales and sharks swim in the open ocean. Others, like giant sponges, hide deep down on the seabed.

Lurking at the bottom of the sea near Japan are **giant spider crabs**. With their claws outstretched they can measure nearly ten feet.

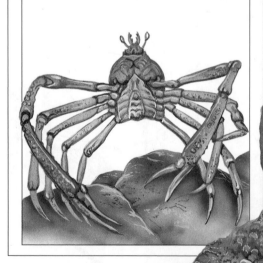

The suckers on a 50 foot **giant squid** measure 4 in. across. But sucker scars on whales have been seen as long as 18 in.!

Trailing deadly poisonous tentacles, **Arctic giant jellyfish** drift in the northern seas. Their tentacles can reach down over 100 feet.

Sharks can detect vibrations and electricity given out by injured creatures over long distances. Some can even taste blood

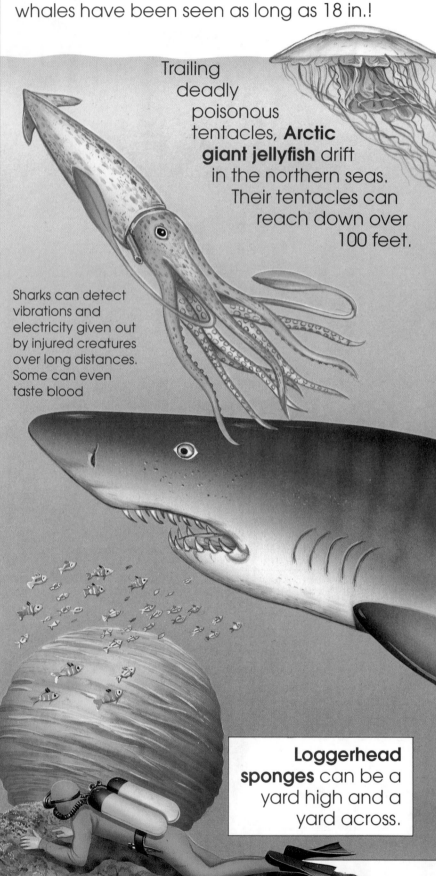

Loggerhead sponges can be a yard high and a yard across.

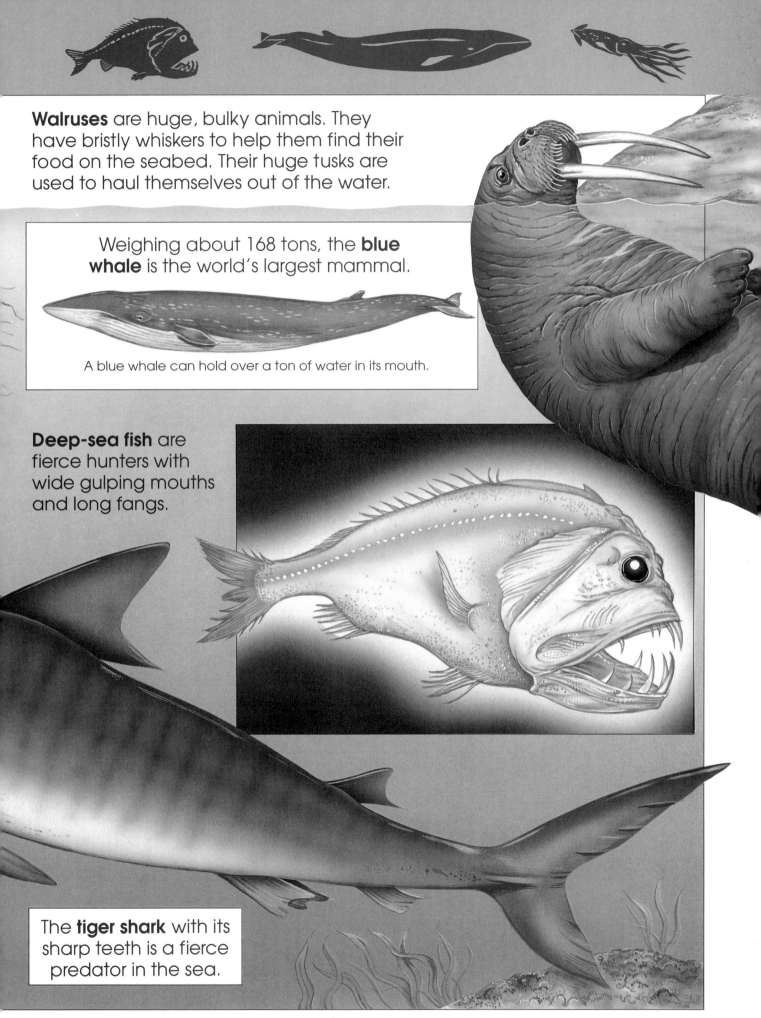

Walruses are huge, bulky animals. They have bristly whiskers to help them find their food on the seabed. Their huge tusks are used to haul themselves out of the water.

Weighing about 168 tons, the **blue whale** is the world's largest mammal.

A blue whale can hold over a ton of water in its mouth.

Deep-sea fish are fierce hunters with wide gulping mouths and long fangs.

The **tiger shark** with its sharp teeth is a fierce predator in the sea.

Monsters in the air

Birds, bats and insects all have wings and can fly. Some are fierce hunters in the air and can grow very large.

Others use their long, needle-sharp claws, called talons, to catch and kill.

Monstrous **robber flies** hunt other insects in the air, piercing them with sharp mouthpieces, and sucking out the contents of their bodies.

Bats are the only mammals that can truly fly. The largest bat is the **flying fox** which can have a wingspan of over 6 feet.

The **Andean condor** is the world's largest bird of prey and can weigh over 25 lbs.

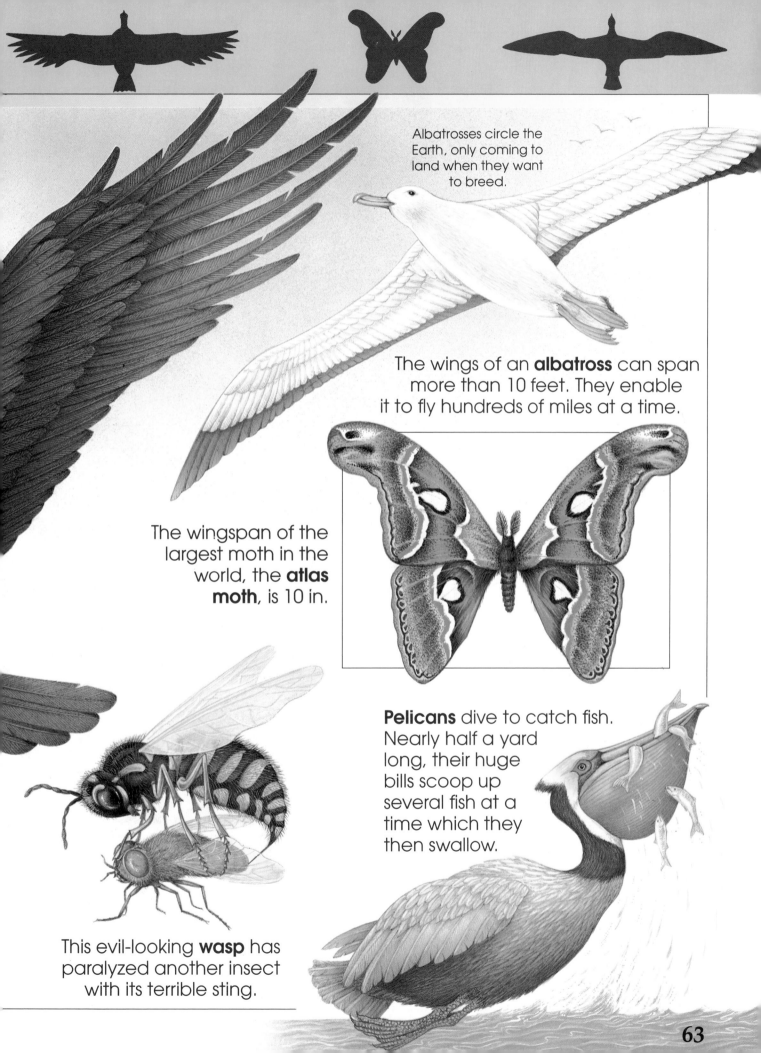

Albatrosses circle the Earth, only coming to land when they want to breed.

The wings of an **albatross** can span more than 10 feet. They enable it to fly hundreds of miles at a time.

The wingspan of the largest moth in the world, the **atlas moth**, is 10 in.

Pelicans dive to catch fish. Nearly half a yard long, their huge bills scoop up several fish at a time which they then swallow.

This evil-looking **wasp** has paralyzed another insect with its terrible sting.

63

Hairy monsters

Monster animals covered with hair can look very strange. They are hairy for many reasons.

Some live in very cold places and need to keep warm. Others use hair for camouflage.

Poisonous hairs protect against attack. Hairs are even used to help some animals breathe underwater.

The hairs on this **Japanese Dictyoploca moth caterpillar** irritate and hurt any predator trying to eat it.

The body of a **porcupine** is covered with special hairs. When frightened the animal rattles these needle-sharp quills.

Some porcupines can even shoot quills out at their enemy.

The "old man of the forest," or **orang-utang**, has very long, golden red hair.

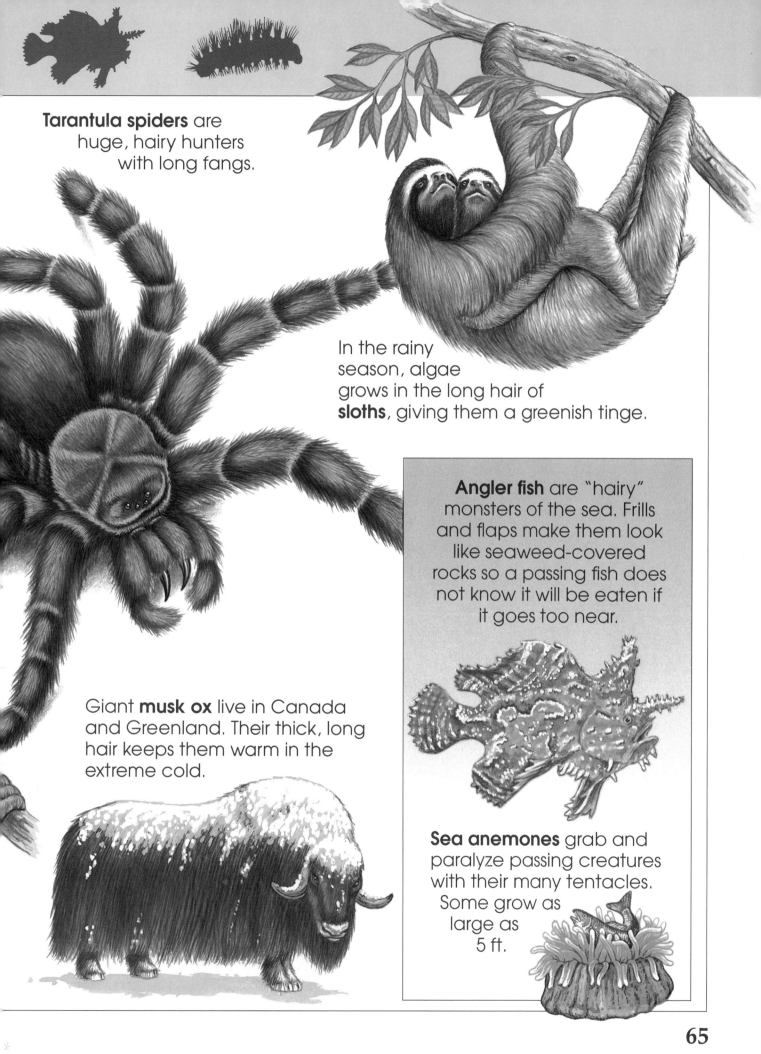

Tarantula spiders are huge, hairy hunters with long fangs.

In the rainy season, algae grows in the long hair of **sloths**, giving them a greenish tinge.

Angler fish are "hairy" monsters of the sea. Frills and flaps make them look like seaweed-covered rocks so a passing fish does not know it will be eaten if it goes too near.

Giant **musk ox** live in Canada and Greenland. Their thick, long hair keeps them warm in the extreme cold.

Sea anemones grab and paralyze passing creatures with their many tentacles. Some grow as large as 5 ft.

Scary monsters

To protect themselves from being attacked or eaten, many animals are monstrous looking.

Some look frightening all the time, while others can make themselves scary when they have to.

Roaring and puffing up their bodies are just some of the methods used.

Death's head hawkmoths can enter beehives and steal honey without being stung.

The strange skull-like markings on the **death's head hawkmoth** give it a deathly appearance.

This is not a fierce prehistoric monster, but a **frilled lizard**. This harmless lizard puts on an impressive display when it is frightened.

Male **stag beetles** have huge, fearsome jaws. They cannot bite with them, but instead joust with other males over females.

Stag beetles use their huge jaws to try and flick their opponent over.

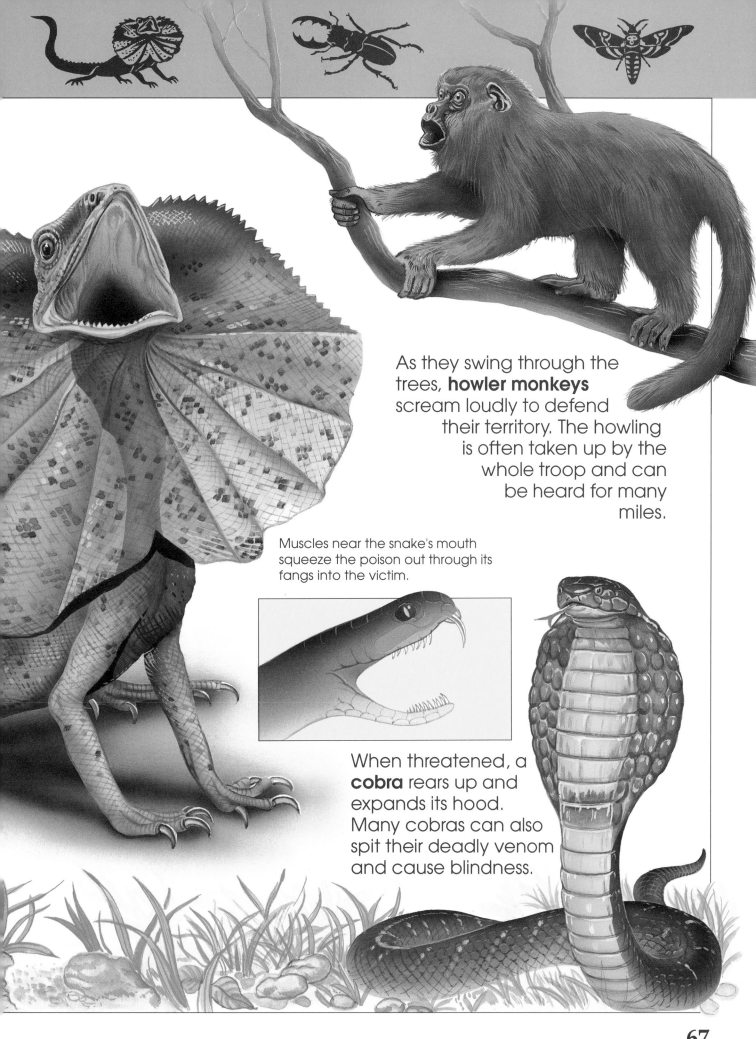

As they swing through the trees, **howler monkeys** scream loudly to defend their territory. The howling is often taken up by the whole troop and can be heard for many miles.

Muscles near the snake's mouth squeeze the poison out through its fangs into the victim.

When threatened, a **cobra** rears up and expands its hood. Many cobras can also spit their deadly venom and cause blindness.

Some monster animals use horrid smells to frighten their predators.

Others live in smelly places or have disgusting habits.

Eating dung and rotting corpses is not particularly nice, but without these animals to clear up, the world would be even smellier!

When a **vampire bat** finds a sleeping animal, it bites into the skin with its razor-sharp front teeth and laps up the blood with its tongue.

Vultures have bald heads and necks. This stops them from getting too dirty with blood as they poke their heads inside a corpse to feed.

Big **dung beetles** carefully roll dung into balls which they hide in tunnels underground for their grubs to eat.

Lampreys cling to other fish with their strange circular mouths surrounded by hooks. They gnaw the flesh and even wriggle into their host's body.

Leeches attach themselves to animals and suck blood causing their bodies to swell. Some can grow as long as 8 in.

Flies are attracted to dead bodies where they feed and lay their eggs. Once hatched, the maggots help to break down the rotten flesh.

Phew! The pungent odor of a **skunk** is disgusting. Skunks spray their scent to mark their territory and put off attackers.

69

Many animals are hunters, preying on other creatures. To catch and kill they have to be cunning, powerful and quick. Most have special teeth, jaws and stings to help catch, hold, kill and devour their victims.

Some of these fierce monsters are quite small. Others grow enormous and will even attack and eat people.

Giant **Colombian horned toads** are aggressive and will attack animals much bigger than themselves - they even bite horses!

Over a thousand people a year are killed by the world's largest and fiercest crocodile, the **Indo-Pacific crocodile**.

A **scorpion** grabs its prey with sharp claws and then bends its tail with its deadly sting over its head and into the victim, killing it with the poison.

Using their razor-sharp pointed teeth, **killer whales** can snatch a seal from a beach by rushing on to the shore on a wave. People stranded on ice floes have also been tipped off and eaten.

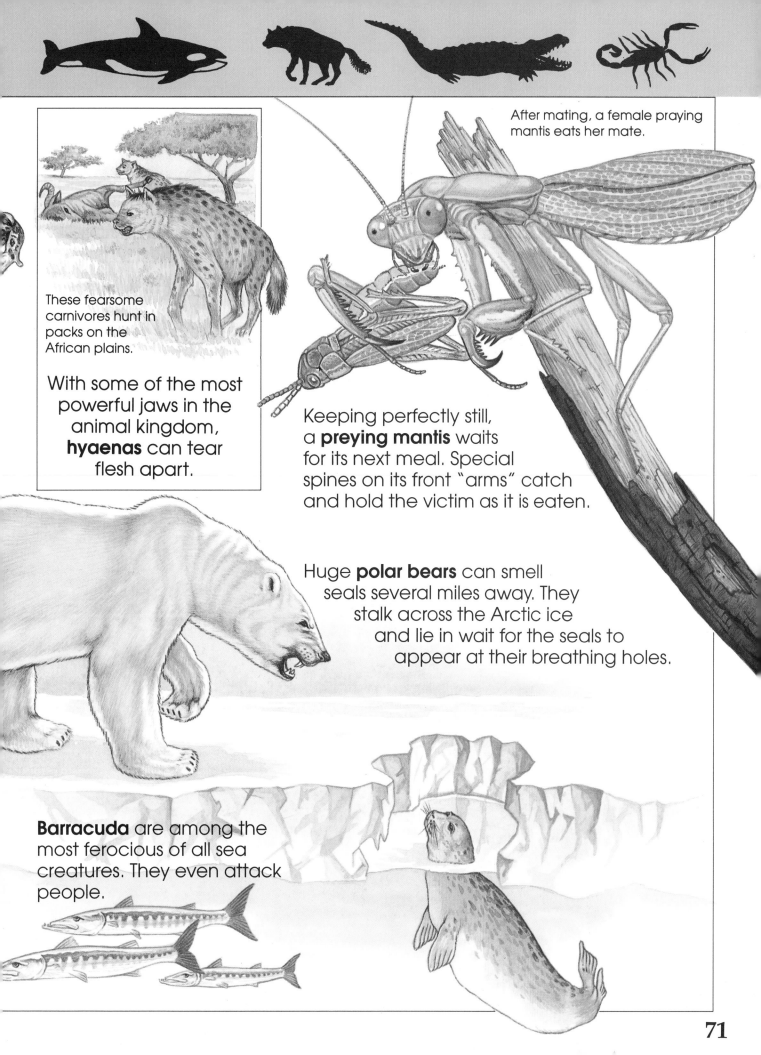

After mating, a female praying mantis eats her mate.

These fearsome carnivores hunt in packs on the African plains.

With some of the most powerful jaws in the animal kingdom, **hyaenas** can tear flesh apart.

Keeping perfectly still, a **preying mantis** waits for its next meal. Special spines on its front "arms" catch and hold the victim as it is eaten.

Huge **polar bears** can smell seals several miles away. They stalk across the Arctic ice and lie in wait for the seals to appear at their breathing holes.

Barracuda are among the most ferocious of all sea creatures. They even attack people.

Fat monsters

Some animals are monstrously fat. Many of them spend most of their time in the water where the weight of their bodies is supported.

Fat bodies can hold a lot of food for times when there is little food around. They can also be used to scare off attackers.

The fat **Vietnamese pot-bellied pig** is kept as a pet in some parts of the world.

Herds of **elephant seals** wallow on the beach. An adult male can weigh almost four tons. When males fight each other they often crush the babies on the beach.

Hippopotamus means "river horse." Although they look fat and clumsy on land, when they are in water they can swim fast.

Hippos use their large teeth for digging up water plants and fighting.

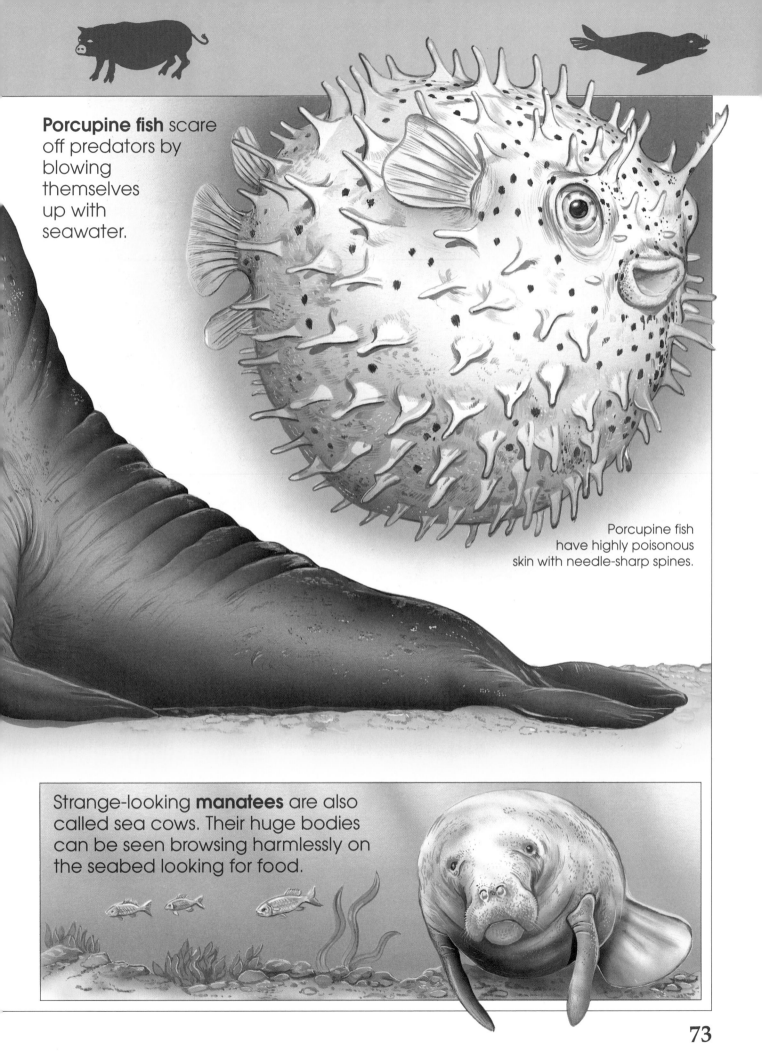

Porcupine fish scare off predators by blowing themselves up with seawater.

Porcupine fish have highly poisonous skin with needle-sharp spines.

Strange-looking **manatees** are also called sea cows. Their huge bodies can be seen browsing harmlessly on the seabed looking for food.

Weird monsters

Some animals are very strange-looking to us. But these monsters are usually the shape they are for a reason.

Everything is made so that it is suited to where it lives so it can survive.

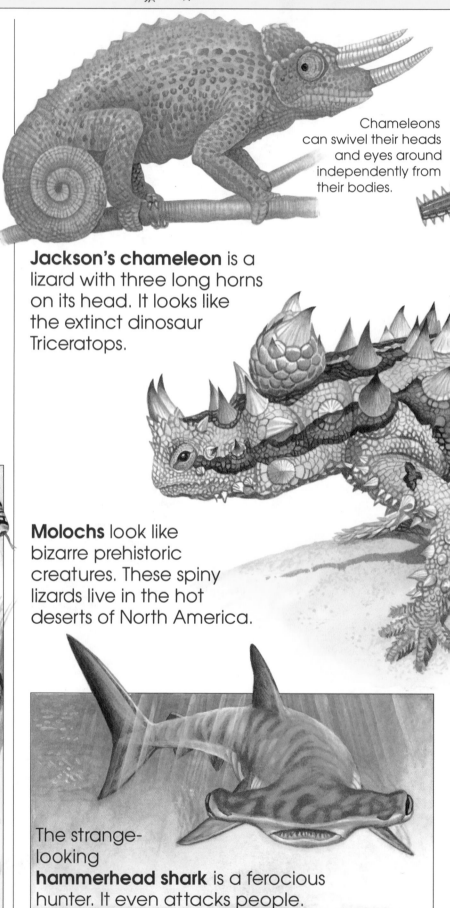

Chameleons can swivel their heads and eyes around independently from their bodies.

Jackson's chameleon is a lizard with three long horns on its head. It looks like the extinct dinosaur Triceratops.

Molochs look like bizarre prehistoric creatures. These spiny lizards live in the hot deserts of North America.

Animals do not usually have two heads, but sometimes they are born. This freak two-headed **kingsnake** was found in California.

The strange-looking **hammerhead shark** is a ferocious hunter. It even attacks people.

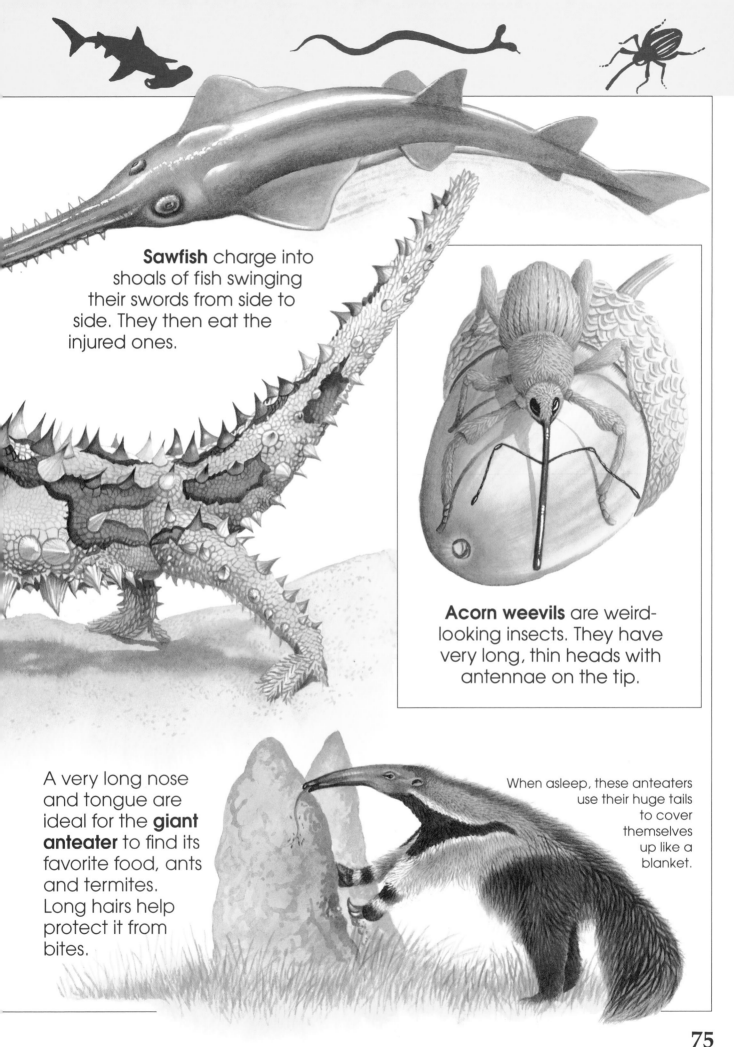

Sawfish charge into shoals of fish swinging their swords from side to side. They then eat the injured ones.

Acorn weevils are weird-looking insects. They have very long, thin heads with antennae on the tip.

A very long nose and tongue are ideal for the **giant anteater** to find its favorite food, ants and termites. Long hairs help protect it from bites.

When asleep, these anteaters use their huge tails to cover themselves up like a blanket.

Deadly monsters

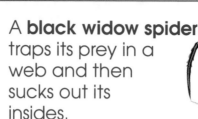

Many animals protect themselves from attack by stinging or biting.

Some animals use poison to stun or kill their prey. Many of these deadly animals have ways of warning others to keep away!

A **black widow spider** traps its prey in a web and then sucks out its insides.

Long, brightly colored spines cover the body of the beautiful but deadly **lion fish**. The sharp spines are coated with toxic mucus and cause terrible pain if touched.

The long trailing tentacles of the **Portuguese Man O'War jellyfish** are highly poisonous. Stinging cells shoot tiny barbed harpoons into anything that touches them.

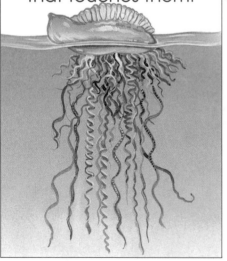

The bright colors of **poison dart frogs** warn predators to leave them alone.

People living in the rainforests of South America smear their blow-pipe darts with the frog's mucus (slime) to poison their prey.

Many **sea urchins** are covered in sharp, poisonous spines for protection. If stepped on the spines can stab and break off in your foot.

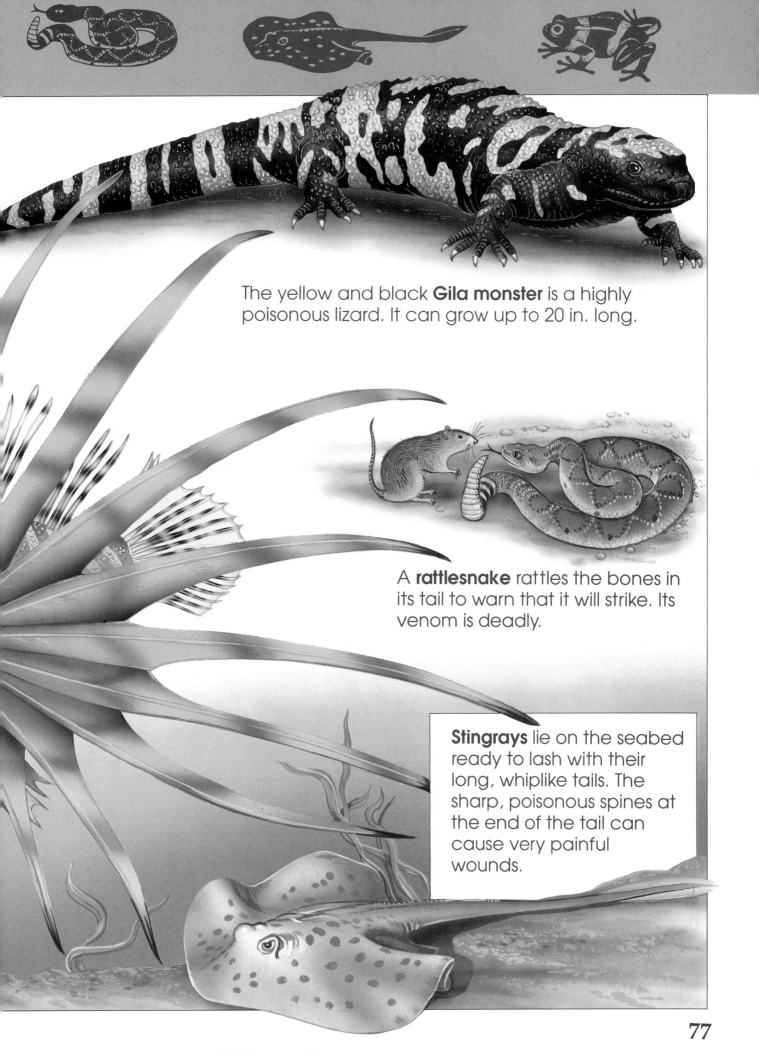

The yellow and black **Gila monster** is a highly poisonous lizard. It can grow up to 20 in. long.

A **rattlesnake** rattles the bones in its tail to warn that it will strike. Its venom is deadly.

Stingrays lie on the seabed ready to lash with their long, whiplike tails. The sharp, poisonous spines at the end of the tail can cause very painful wounds.

Some animals are only frightening and dangerous in large numbers.

Some, like bees, live together in groups to help each other. Others, like wolves, hunt in packs.

Some animals only group together in masses at certain times.

In some parts of the world, plagues of flying **locusts** can darken the sky, eating every green plant they land on.

Hornets live as a colony, nesting inside hollow trees. They use their huge jaws and deadly sting to hunt.

A colony of **army ants** marching through the forest will eat everything in its way - even small animals.

Millions of **mosquitoes** often breed together. The females must have a blood meal before they can lay their eggs. A person can lose nearly a pint of blood to these insects if they are not protected.

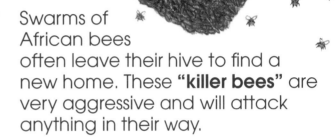

Swarms of African bees often leave their hive to find a new home. These **"killer bees"** are very aggressive and will attack anything in their way.

African wild dogs live in packs of up to 60. By circling their prey and dashing in and biting it, the victim is soon weakened and killed.

Hunting together in packs, **wolves** can catch and kill large animals. They usually attack the weak and sick, but rarely people.

Rare monsters

Many animals are becoming rare. Some have already become extinct and will never be seen again outside a museum.

People kill animals for their skin, fur, feathers and horns. We also destroy the places where they live.

The largest **false scorpion** in Europe lives under the bark of dead trees. It is now extremely rare and only found in ancient forests.

On Maria Island in the West Indies lives the world's rarest snake, the **St. Lucia racer**. There are less than 100 left.

Racers are large, fast snakes which strike repeatedly with their heads when attacked, tearing the flesh.

Wildlife parks and zoos do important work trying to save animals from extinction. The last wild **Californian condor** was captured so it could breed under protection.

Trap door spiders in Southeast Asia are the rarest spiders. They use their jaws to dig holes, leaving a hinged lid at the entrance. When a victim comes near, the spider opens the lid, grabs its prey, and pulls it underground.

Javan rhinoceros hide in the rainforest. Sadly their forest home is being cut down and the animals hunted for their horn.

The **red wolf** has become extinct in the wild. Breeding in captivity has produced over 100.

On the island of St. Helena, off the coast of Africa, lives the large and very rare **giant earwig**.

Hunting and pollution has reduced the number of **Chinese alligators** to less than 100 in the wild.

Millions of years ago, all kinds of strange monstrous animals roamed the Earth.

There were no people around when the dinosaurs ruled the world.

When people appeared they cut down forests and hunted animals. Some of the larger species were driven into extinction. Today, people still kill and threaten many animals.

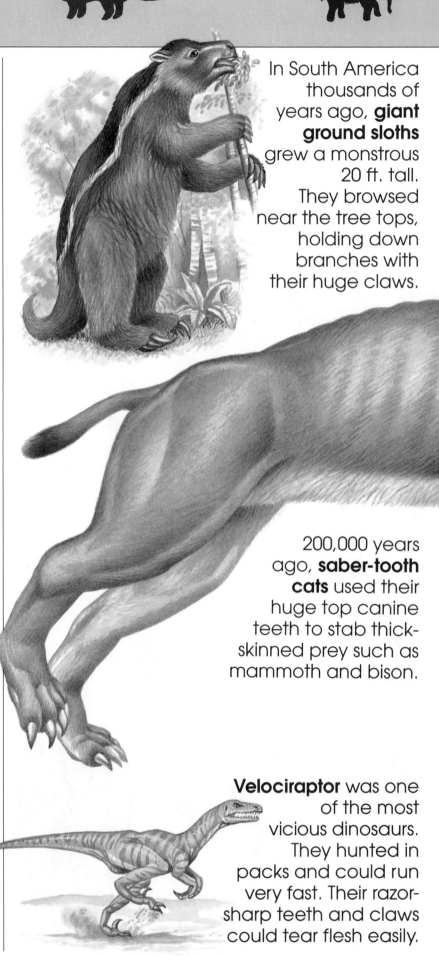

In South America thousands of years ago, **giant ground sloths** grew a monstrous 20 ft. tall. They browsed near the tree tops, holding down branches with their huge claws.

200,000 years ago, **saber-tooth cats** used their huge top canine teeth to stab thick-skinned prey such as mammoth and bison.

Velociraptor was one of the most vicious dinosaurs. They hunted in packs and could run very fast. Their razor-sharp teeth and claws could tear flesh easily.

Quetzalcoatlus' wings were made of skin like those of bats today.

97 million years ago, **quetzalcoatlus** soared through the air on wings spanning 40 feet.

Giant Irish deer grew antlers nearly 13 feet across. They died out 2,500 years ago.

Mammoths are one of the largest land mammals to have lived. They grew over 13 ft. tall and had woolly coats and huge tusks.

The giant **moa** of New Zealand was the tallest bird that ever existed. It stood over 10 feet tall.

People destroyed the moa's habitat and hunted it, so that by 1800 it was extinct.

Hyaenodon must have been a fearsome hunter and scavenger. Its skull was 26 in. long and full of needle-sharp teeth.

What is a warrior?

Warriors were men or women who fought bravely. Often they were not paid to fight, but fought because they believed they were right.

Warriors did not win all of the time. Some of the most famous warriors are those who lost, but who fought with great courage.

Byrhtnoth was an English earl. In 991, he and all his men died fighting a Viking force near Maldon in Essex. They fought so bravely that a poem, called "The Battle of Maldon," was written about their heroic struggle.

Shaka was the king of the Zulu, a large tribe in South Africa. In 1816, Shaka trained the Zulu warriors in new battle tactics. By 1850 the Zulus had defeated all neighboring tribes. In 1879 the Zulus wiped out a British regiment before being defeated by the British at Rorke's Drift and Kambula.

Warriors used different types of **weapons**. Early warriors used clubs and rocks, while more modern warriors used rifles and cannons.

The Assyrians conquered a large empire in the Near East about 3,000 years ago.

Ashanti warriors fought in the dense forests of West Africa about 100 years ago.

The **Maori** live in New Zealand. They used to live in great tribes which fought wars with each other, and later, with European settlers. Sometimes whole tribes were killed in battle as they refused to surrender. Although the Europeans accepted the Maori as equals in 1840, wars continued for many years.

In 336 B.C. Alexander the Great became King of Macedonia (in northern Greece). He was only 20 years old. Within 13 years he had become the most powerful ruler in the world.

He defeated armies larger than his own using clever new tactics and weapons.

Alexander's horse was called **Bucephalus**. According to legend, Alexander, who was only 12 years old at the time, was the only person who could control him. When Bucephalus died Alexander named a town in India, Bucephala, in honor of him.

The Battle of Gaugamela in 331 B.C. was Alexander's greatest victory. He defeated a Persian army of 150,000 men with his army of only 35,000 Macedonians. The battle was won when Alexander led a cavalry charge which scattered the Persian infantry.

The cavalry led the attacks in battle. They were used to open gaps in the enemy army. The horsemen would charge forward, followed by the infantry.

King Darius, was Alexander's biggest enemy. He became ruler of the Persian Empire in 336 B.C. after murdering the previous three rulers. Darius was a successful warrior who defeated many enemies, but he lost two major battles to Alexander. In 330 B.C. Darius was murdered by his cousin.

Infantry in Alexander's army used a very long spear called a **sarissa**. Each sarissa was 15 feet long.

By 323 B.C. Alexander's Empire was the largest in the world at that time. He wanted to join all the kingdoms he had conquered to form one country. After Alexander died, his generals divided the empire between themselves. Within 150 years the empire no longer existed.

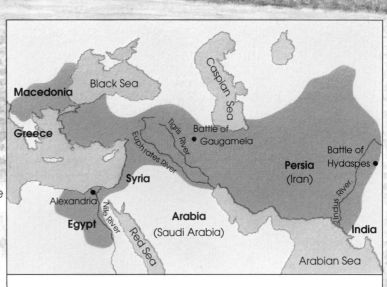

The Empire of Alexander the Great

Alexander reached **India** in 326 B.C. He defeated a local king, Porus, at the Battle of the Hydaspes (modern-day Jhelum) and added new territories to his empire.

Attila was the king of the Huns, a warlike tribe feared in Europe and Asia. He became sole King in 444 after murdering his elder brother, Breda, who was joint King at the time.

Attila organized the Huns into a powerful army. By conquering neighboring kingdoms he built up a large empire. Soon, he became known as "the scourge of God."

The Huns came from central Asia in about 370 and settled in what is now Hungary. Attila led his tribe in wars that ranged across Greece, southern Russia, Germany and France.

The Huns loved gold - during one raid into Greece they stole over 2,000 lbs!

In 453 Attila died suddenly after a feast on his wedding day. He was buried with his treasure. The slaves who buried him were all killed to keep the location secret. Without Attila's leadership, the Huns were easily defeated by their enemies.

Attila arrived in Italy in 452 and captured many cities. Pope Leo I persuaded him to spare Rome from attack.

Venice is a city in northern Italy surrounded by the sea. It was founded by Romans fleeing from Attila. The escaping Romans were safe on the islands of Venice as the Huns did not have a navy.

Horses were the Huns' most important possession. They used them to look after their large herds of cattle and sheep. They also fought on horseback, using spears and bows to attack their enemies.

Hun warriors scarred their faces with knives to make themselves look fierce to frighten their enemies.

The Huns used the **lasso** as a weapon. One Hun would catch an enemy with a lasso, allowing another warrior to kill the captive.

The Roman Empire began around 753 B.C. and lasted over 1,000 years until A.D. 476. It covered all the lands around the Mediterranean, and much of Europe.

These lands were conquered and policed by the Roman Army. The Romans defeated many enemies because of their superior weapons and tactics.

The Romans were excellent builders as well as warriors. They made roads to move their armies from one place to another, and built forts and walls to keep out invaders. **Hadrian's Wall**, in northern England, was built to keep enemies from invading England from Scotland.

The legionary was the most important type of Roman warrior. Legionaries wore strong suits of armor and fought on foot. They were grouped together in a century, made up of 80 legionaries led by an officer known as a centurion.

Roman legionaries marched and fought together in a large group of 5,200 legionaries, called a **legion**.

Horatius was a legendary early Roman warrior. In about 670 B.C. a large Etruscan army (from northern Italy) attacked Rome. The bridge leading to Rome across the Tiber River had to be cut down to stop the Etruscan invasion. Horatius fought the Etruscans single-handedly to give the Romans time to cut down the bridge. Rome was saved and Horatius survived to be declared a hero.

Mark Antony was a famous general. He fell in love with Cleopatra, the Queen of Egypt, and gave her land belonging to Rome. This led to a civil war with the Roman authorities which Mark Antony lost. Later, he took his own life.

Legionaries arranged themselves in special formations when attacking the enemy. The "tortoise" protected legionaries from arrows and spears. The "wedge" was used to smash through enemy ranks.

A bronze eagle was the symbol of a legion and it was carried into battle. Romans thought it was an insult to the gods if the eagle were captured by the enemy.

The Roman Empire was very large and had many enemies. There were tribes fighting their Roman conquerors, and armies from other empires trying to invade Rome.

The **Celts** were divided into many different tribes, who lived right across Europe from Scotland to Serbia. They were often a war-like people, who rode chariots into battle and sometimes sang as they fought. After a battle, the Celts would cut off the heads of their dead enemies and hold a feast to celebrate.

Vercingetorix was the Celtic leader of Gaul (modern-day France). He fought against the Roman general Julius Caesar in 52 B.C. After several battles, Vercingetorix was captured and beheaded.

Hannibal was a famous nobleman from Carthage (in modern-day Tunisia). He was one of Rome's most dangerous enemies. In 218 B.C. he led his army, along with 38 elephants, from Spain through France and across the Alps into Italy. He won many battles there, including the defeat of 50,000 Romans at Cannae. He never reached Rome and was forced to return to Carthage.

Spartacus was a slave who escaped from a gladiator school in 73 B.C. Thousands of other slaves ran away to join him. Spartacus led them through Italy stealing and burning everything they could find. He was defeated and died in battle at Lucania in 71 B.C. The 6,000 prisoners captured by the Romans were all crucified.

Boudicca was Queen of the Iceni, a tribe from East Anglia, in England. In A.D. 61 she led her tribe in revolt after she and her daughters had been ill-treated by the Romans, who had also increased the taxes. Boudicca's Celtic warriors destroyed Colchester, London and St. Albans before being beaten by the Romans. Rather than surrender, she poisoned herself.

Arminius was a German chief. In A.D. 9 he and his warriors trapped three Roman legions in a swampy forest and killed them all.

Masada was a fortress in Palestine held by 1,000 Jewish rebels in A.D. 72-73. After a two-year siege by 15,000 Romans, all but seven of the Jews, including the children, committed suicide rather than surrender.

93

Ireland was never conquered by the Romans. Instead, Ireland remained a land ruled by Celtic chiefs.

Although there was a High King of Ireland most tribes continued to fight each other.

Irish kings and chiefs often lived in well defended **strongholds**. The remains of the Rock of Cashel in Tipperary County are a good example of an ancient Irish stronghold. The rock was home to the kings of Munster.

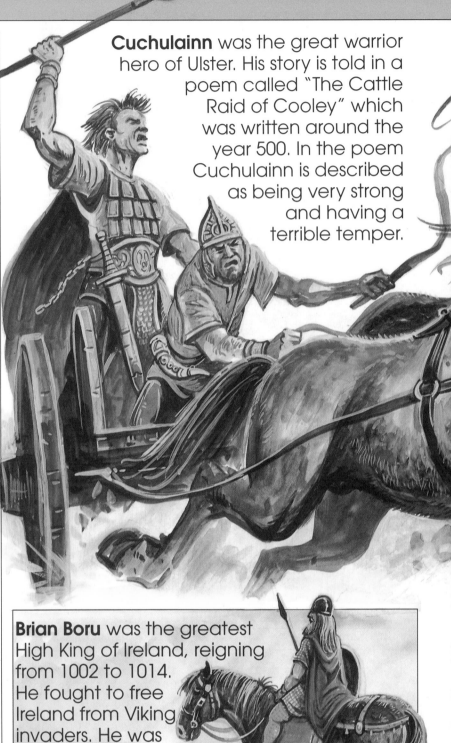

Cuchulainn was the great warrior hero of Ulster. His story is told in a poem called "The Cattle Raid of Cooley" which was written around the year 500. In the poem Cuchulainn is described as being very strong and having a terrible temper.

Brian Boru was the greatest High King of Ireland, reigning from 1002 to 1014. He fought to free Ireland from Viking invaders. He was murdered by a fleeing band of Vikings after finally defeating the Viking army at Clontarf.

Women are important characters in Irish mythology. The legendary **Queen Maeve** of Connaught led an army against Ulster, and fought against Cuchulainn.

Fionn mac Cumhaill was the legendary hero of Leinster. According to the stories told about him, he led a band of brave young warriors who loved to hunt. These warriors were known as the Fianna. The Fianna rebelled against Cairbre, High King of Ireland, in an argument about hunting lands. The Fianna were destroyed in the following battle.

Strongbow was the nickname of Richard Fitzgilbert, a Norman lord. He came to Ireland in 1170 to help Dermot MacMurrogh, King of Leinster, become High King. After Dermot's death, Strongbow grabbed his lands for himself. Soon, other Norman and English knights came to Ireland and took over much of the country.

The Vikings came from Norway, Denmark and Sweden. They raided northern Europe and even traveled to North America and Italy.

A carved head from a Viking ship

The Vikings were also merchants, trading with Arabs and people from Asia. They sold furs, ivory and slaves and bought silk, spices and gold.

Weapons were made by skilled craftspeople. Axes and swords were favorite weapons. Valuable swords were passed from father to son. They were given frightening names such as "blood-sucker" or "man-killer!"

Raids were carried out by warriors in longships. As many as 100 longships would take part in a single raid. The Vikings would land, capture as much money, food, cattle and valuables as possible and sail away again.

Longships were narrow boats which could be up to 100 feet in length. They were not very heavy and were very quick through the water as they had oars as well as a large sail. Some longships had dragon heads carved on to them to make them look fiercer.

Sweyn Forkbeard was the greatest Viking of his time. He built a large empire based around the North Sea. He was King of Denmark and Norway, and in 1013 he became King of England.

The Vikings started to settle in the places that they had raided in the past. There were **settlements** in northern England, northern France and southern Ireland. Remains of these settlements can still be seen in York, in England, and Dublin, in Ireland.

Eric Bloodaxe became King of Northumberland, in England, in 948. He had been forced to flee from Norway after murdering two of his brothers to become sole King of Norway. Eric was driven out of England in 948, and again in 954. He was killed later that year on returning to England.

Viking warriors believed that when they died they would go to **Valhalla**, the banquet hall of the gods. Viking chiefs and famous warriors would often be buried with their boats and their favorite possessions when they died. Sometimes the body would be placed on the deck of the boat and burned.

Genghis Khan

Genghis Khan united all the Mongol tribes of central Asia and created the largest land empire the world has ever seen.

His empire relied upon ferocious mounted warriors and a reign of terror, which left cities burnt to the ground and millions of people dead.

Each warrior had two bows, 100 arrows, a lance and a sword. Arrows came in several designs. Some were specially shaped to travel long distances, others to pierce metal armor. One type of arrow was fitted with a whistle to frighten enemy troops.

Genghis Khan's real name was **Temujin**. He was born in 1167, the son of a minor tribal chief. His father was poisoned by a neighboring tribe, but Temujin became leader himself. He acted very bravely in battle and at a meeting of the Mongol tribes in 1206 he was given the title "Genghis Khan," which means "Great Ruler."

Genghis Khan was also the ruler of the **Merkit**, **Tartar**, **Kirghiz** and **Naiman** tribes.

The Mongols were a very ruthless tribe. When they captured a city they would put women, young children and the craftsmen who made weapons to one side. Then they would kill everybody else. When the city of **Merv** was captured, about 700,000 people were killed.

The invasion of **China** began in 1211 when the Mongols broke through the Great Wall. In 1215, Peking was captured and northern China was conquered.

The Mongols fought on horseback. Their horses were small and strong. They were bred to withstand the cold and heat and were trained to keep calm in battle.

The **Mongol Empire** was the largest land empire ever known. By 1279 it stretched from Hungary to Korea and included most of Asia.

Russia

Arabia

Arabian Sea

India

China

Pacific Ocean

The Mongol Empire

The Crusades were wars between Christians and Muslims. There were seven Crusades between the years 1095 and 1300.

The name "Crusader" comes from the Latin word for cross. The Christian warriors were called Crusaders because they wore a cross as their badge.

Assassins were sent into Crusader camps by the Muslims to murder important leaders.

Richard the Lionheart was a King of England who led the Third Crusade in 1190. At the battle of Arsouf, in 1191, Richard defeated a large Muslim army and in the following year, he defeated another Muslim army at Jaffa. He led the Christian attack himself and acted with great bravery. Richard forced the Muslims to agree to a truce that allowed Christians to visit Jerusalem.

Warrior monks fought in the Crusades. These were special monks who made promises to God to fight against the Muslims. The Templar Order was the most famous group of warrior monks. The order was founded in 1118 to protect pilgrims going to Jerusalem. Other orders included the Hospitallers, the Trufac and the Teutonic.

Saladin was the great Muslim leader of the 1100s. In 1175 he became Sultan (ruler) of Damascus and went on to unite the Muslims. He defeated the Crusaders in many important battles and stopped them from taking over Jerusalem.

El Cid was the nickname given to Rodrigo di Vivar. He was a great Spanish warrior who fought against the Muslims. El Cid means "The Champion." In 1094 he defeated the Muslims and captured the city of Valencia. He ruled it until his death in battle in 1099.

The Kingdom of Outremer

The Crusaders set up their own kingdom in Palestine called **Outremer**. The name means "Beyond the Sea," because Palestine is across the Mediterranean Ocean from Rome, the Christians' headquarters.

101

Sitting Bull

Sitting Bull was the greatest leader of the Sioux people. He united the Sioux tribes.

With the help of the Blackfeet, Cheyenne and Arapahoe tribes, he led a war against the American settlers.

Warriors like the Sioux fought on horseback. They were armed with spears, bows and arrows, or guns bought from the white settlers.

The **first Indian War** began in 1608 when English settlers fought the Powhatan tribe in Virginia. The war ended in 1613 when the Indian princess Pocahontas married an Englishman.

Red Cloud was chief of one of the Sioux tribes. He fought against the American army to stop them from building forts and a road across land belonging to the Sioux and Cheyenne tribes. The war lasted for two years, from 1865 until 1867, when the government was forced to leave the tribes' land. Red Cloud made peace with the settlers, but continued to defend the rights of his people with many visits to the government in Washington.

When **gold** was found on Sioux land, the American government ordered Sitting Bull to move his people to a new reservation 235 mi. away. Sitting Bull refused to move and war broke out between the government and the Sioux.

In 1876, General Custer was sent with the 7th Cavalry to attack the Indian camp at **Little Big Horn**. Custer sent part of his troops to attack the Indian rear, and charged forward with the remaining troops. He rode straight into a trap set by Sitting Bull and another chief, called Crazy Horse. Custer and all his men were killed.

Geronimo was the leader of the Apache, who lived in the deserts of the U.S.-Mexico border. In 1859, the Apache were attacked by Mexicans. After this the Apache fought a war against all whites. For many years Geronimo led his warriors in a brutal conflict until he surrendered in 1886.

The Orient is the name given to the lands to the east of the Mediterranean Sea, especially those in eastern Asia, such as China or Japan.

Many ruthless warriors have fought each other across this vast area of land.

Samurai warriors came from Japan. They were highly trained fighters who were loyal to their local lord. All Samurai followed a strict set of rules, known as Bushido. These rules encouraged the Samurai to be brave, honest and live a simple life. If a Samurai broke the rules of Bushido or lost a batle, he had to kill himself. This was known as seppuku.

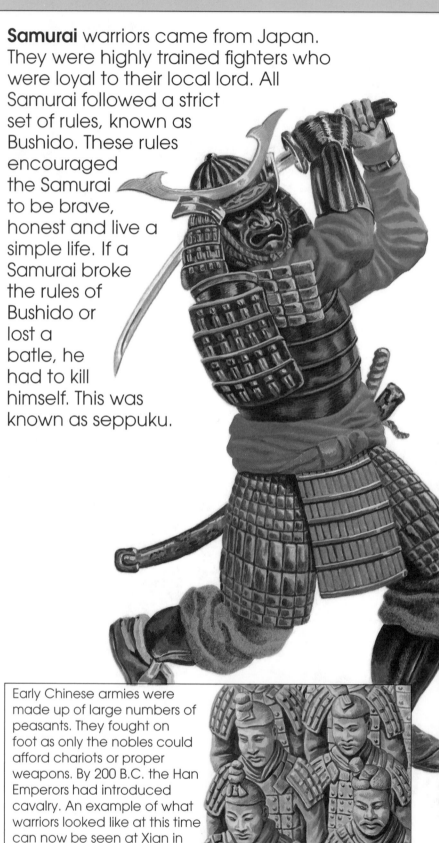

The **Great Wall of China** was built by the Emperor Shih Huang-ti around 220 B.C. It was designed to protect China from invasions from the north. It is over 3,728 mi. long and wide enough to drive a chariot along the top. Today it is a major tourist attraction.

Early Chinese armies were made up of large numbers of peasants. They fought on foot as only the nobles could afford chariots or proper weapons. By 200 B.C. the Han Emperors had introduced cavalry. An example of what warriors looked like at this time can now be seen at Xian in China after the discovery of 6,000 life-size terracotta models of the Emperor Shih Huang-ti's army.

Timur the Lame, or Tamerlane as he was known in Europe, was the ruthless leader of the Tartar warriors from southern Asia. He was born in 1336 in Samarkand, which is in modern-day Tajikistan. By 1399, he had conquered or made treaties with all of central Asia, and invaded Russia and India. Timur was a cruel person who slaughtered thousands of people. He would build great pyramids of skulls from the people he killed before taking their treasure back to Samarkand.

An Lu-Shan was a Turkish warrior who became ruler of China. As a young man, he was a cavalry commander in the Chinese army. He won many victories against the enemies of China and was soon commander of the entire northern army. In 756, thinking the Emperor had ordered his death, An Lu-Shan attacked China. He overthrew the Emperor and became ruler of China. He was murdered one year later by a servant.

Freedom fighters are warriors who try to free their country from the rule of a foreign nation.

Most freedom fighters work in small groups rather than with a large army. Sometimes they win and their country is freed. Other freedom fighters fail but they become heroes and inspire others to follow their ideas.

Joan of Arc led the French in a war against the English. In 1429 England ruled most of France. Joan, a young farmer's daughter, persuaded the Dauphin (the French heir to the throne) to let her fight with a small army. Joan amazed the troops with her bravery and leadership. She was captured and executed by the English in 1431. Thousands of French people were inspired by Joan and within a few years France was free.

Simon Bolívar fought to free South Americans from the Spanish Empire. In 1810 Venezuela threw out the Spanish governor. Bolivar took command of the rebel army and won many victories. In 1821 Spain accepted defeat. Bolívar then went on to lead rebels in Colombia, Peru, Ecuador and Bolivia.

Francois Toussaint L'Ouverture was a black slave who led the slaves of Haiti to freedom. In 1791 he led a slave revolt against the foreign rulers of the island and by 1797 he was ruler of Haiti. Toussant outlawed slavery and brought in many humane laws.

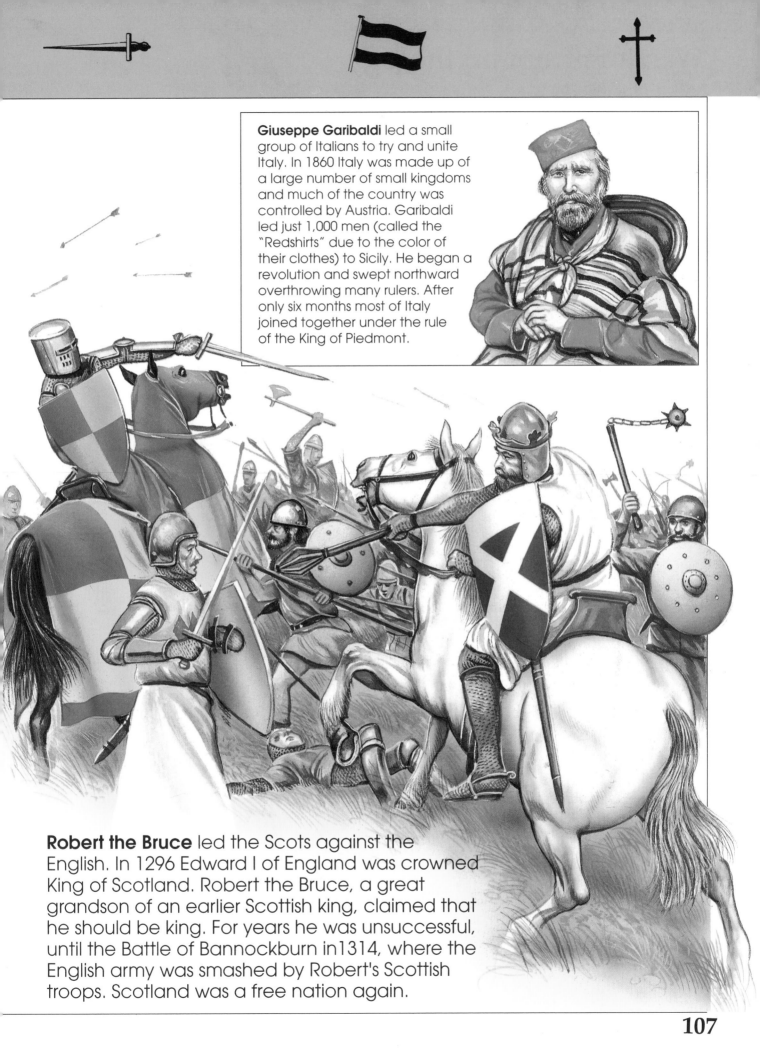

Giuseppe Garibaldi led a small group of Italians to try and unite Italy. In 1860 Italy was made up of a large number of small kingdoms and much of the country was controlled by Austria. Garibaldi led just 1,000 men (called the "Redshirts" due to the color of their clothes) to Sicily. He began a revolution and swept northward overthrowing many rulers. After only six months most of Italy joined together under the rule of the King of Piedmont.

Robert the Bruce led the Scots against the English. In 1296 Edward I of England was crowned King of Scotland. Robert the Bruce, a great grandson of an earlier Scottish king, claimed that he should be king. For years he was unsuccessful, until the Battle of Bannockburn in 1314, where the English army was smashed by Robert's Scottish troops. Scotland was a free nation again.

Mythical warriors appear in legends from many countries.

Although fantastic stories are told about these warriors, the legends are often based upon the lives of real people.

Gilgamesh was a legendary hero of Ancient Persia in about 2000 B.C. In the legend, Gilgamesh was a king who goes on a long journey to try to discover the meaning of life. It is thought that Gilgamesh was a famous warrior-king of Uruk in about 2500 B.C.

Horus was an Ancient Egyptian god. It is thought that the many stories told about his conflict with the god Seth refer to ancient tribal conflicts before the first pharaoh united Egypt in about 2800 B.C.

The Ancient Greeks and Persians told stories of female warriors called **Amazons**. The Amazons were a race of war-like women who raided other countries to capture gold and men. In fact, the Amazon legend was probably based on a real-life tribe called Sarmatians, who lived near the Black Sea between 800 B.C. and 300 B.C. Sarmatian women had equal rights with men and fought in battles. This seemed very strange to the Greeks and Persians of the time and led to the stories about the Amazons.

Jason was a prince from Thessaly in Greece. Storytellers would tell tales of how Jason had to visit many distant countries with the help of a band of warriors called the Argonauts before he could be king. The stories are probably based on the journeys of several different Thessalians. Sailors from Thessaly visited many countries in search of trade.

King Arthur is a legendary warrior of Britain. According to legend, Arthur was a great king who led a band of noble and gentle knights. The knights sat around a round table so that no one would appear to be more important than any of the others by sitting at the head of the table. In fact, Arthur was probably a Celtic warrior who fought against the Anglo-Saxons (who invaded Britain after the Romans left). He is thought to have been killed at the Battle of Camlann in about 515.

Sigurd was a great hero warrior of the Vikings. He was the last of the Volsung tribe and had many adventures, like fighting a dragon and finding treasure. Nobody has been able to discover who the character of Sigurd was based upon.

Europe

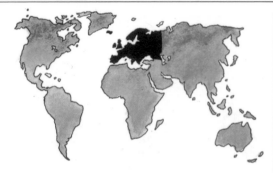

Europe is the second smallest continent in the world. About 700 million people live there, so it is very crowded compared to other regions.

Europe has ocean to the north, south and west. To the east, it borders the continent of Asia.

The Ural Mountains separate Europe from Asia.

There are more than 40 countries in Europe. The continent stretches from inside the Arctic Circle down to the Mediterranean Sea. Each country has its own government, capital city, languages and customs.

Key facts

Size: 4,062,158 sq. mi. (7% of the world's land surface)
Smallest country: Vatican City (.17 sq. mi.)
Largest country: Russia (1,757,141 sq. mi. of it is in Europe)
Longest river: Volga (2,194 mi.)
Highest mountain: Mount Elbrus (18,482 ft.) in the Caucasus mountain range

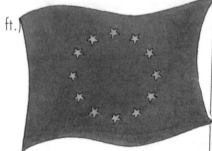

The flag of the EC

Countries

Twelve European countries are members of the EC, or the European Community. The members work together to make laws in areas such as farming, industry and finance.

The group of countries in the west of the European continent is sometimes known as Western Europe.

Many countries in the east of Europe are changing. The former Soviet Union has now divided into fifteen separate republics.

Landscape

Europe's landscape is very varied. In the far north you can see lots of forests and lakes. In central parts there are meadows and low hills. The south has some high mountain ranges and wide plains.

Western Europe's highest mountain range is the Alps, which stretches across the top of Italy. Alpine peaks are snowy all year. The Alps are very popular for skiing vacations.

Yassoo!
Greek

Ola!
Spanish

Halloj!
Danish

Zdras-vuytya!
Russian

Economy

There are lots of industries in Europe. Goods are imported and exported through the many seaports. Farming of all kinds is also important.

Europe has many busy seaports

Main industries

Fishing
Timber
Farming
Textiles

Steel
Engineering
Mining

Weather

In Scandinavia it is cold much of the time. In Eastern Europe the winters are very cold, but the summers are warm. Over Western Europe the summers are warm, the winters are cool and rain falls throughout the year.

Map key

1 Albania
2 Andorra
3 Austria
4 Belarus
5 Belgium
6 Bosnia & Herzegovina
7 Bulgaria
8 Croatia
9 Czech Republic
10 Denmark
11 Estonia
12 Finland
13 France
14 Germany
15 Gibraltar
16 Greece
17 Hungary
18 Iceland
19 Ireland
20 Italy
21 Latvia
22 Liechtenstein
23 Lithuania
24 Luxembourg
25 Macedonia
26 Malta
27 Moldova
28 Monaco
29 Netherlands
30 Norway
31 Poland
32 Portugal
33 Romania
34 Russia
(34) Kaliningrad
35 San Marino
36 Slovakia
37 Slovenia
38 Spain
39 Sweden
40 Switzerland
41 Ukraine
42 United Kingdom
43 Vatican City
44 Yugoslavia

Map of Europe

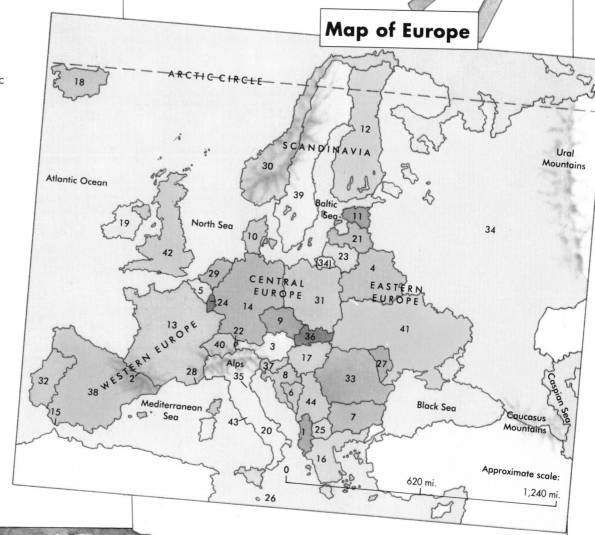

111

United Kingdom

The United Kingdom lies off Europe's north-west coast. It is made up of four countries.

Key facts

Size: 94,226 sq. mi.
Population: More than 57 million
Currency: Pound sterling
Main language: English
Also called: Britain, U.K.

England, Scotland, Northern Ireland and Wales make up the U.K.

English flag   **Scottish flag**

Welsh flag   **Northern Irish flag**

Capital city: London. About 6.4 million people live here. London is the center of business and government.

A London bus

Landscape: The highest mountains are in Wales and Scotland. The tallest is Ben Nevis (4,406 ft.) in Scotland. The longest river is the Severn (468 mi.). It flows from Wales into England.

Industries

Chemicals
Electronics
Textiles
Heavy machinery
Oil

Ben Nevis

Places to visit: There are lots of historical sites, ancient cities and towns. Britain is famous for its royal palaces and stately homes.

The Tower of London, Britain's most popular tourist attraction

France

France is one of the largest countries on the European continent.

Key facts

Size: 211,207 sq. mi.
Population: Over 56 million
Currency: French franc
Main language: French

Capital city: Paris. This is a world center of fashion and art. It has many famous art galleries and museums.

The Eiffel Tower is in Paris. It is made of iron and stands 984 ft. high. You can travel to the top by elevator.

Eiffel Tower

Landscape: France has many different kinds of scenery, with spectacular mountains, pretty river valleys and sunny beaches. Mont Blanc, on the Italian border, is the highest mountain (15,772 ft.). The longest river is the Loire (653 mi.).

Grapes are grown for wine

Industries

Farming
Wine
Tourism
Fashion
Vehicles
Chemicals

A vineyard

Places to visit: You can ski in the Alps, swim in the Mediterranean or visit many historic chateaux. EuroDisney™ is near Paris.

The royal château at Versailles

Spain

Spain is in south-west Europe. It is the third largest country on the continent.

Key facts

Size: 194,896 sq. mi.
Population: Over 38 million
Currency: Peseta
Main language: Spanish

The Royal Palace

Capital city: Madrid. This is a famous center of culture with many theaters, cinemas and opera houses.

Landscape: Spain is a mountainous country. In the center there is a vast, high plateau. The highest mountain is Mt. Mulhacen (11,440 ft.). The longest river is the Tagus (626 mi.).

The Sierra Nevada mountains

Places to visit: There are many historic cities and palaces built by the Moors, who invaded from Africa in 711. In the south there are sunny beaches.

The Alhambra, a Moorish palace near Granada

Industries

Tourism
Wine
Farming
Vehicles
Chemicals
Electronics

Germany

Germany borders nine other countries. In 1990, East and West Germany joined to become one country.

Berlin

Key facts

Size: 137,743 sq. mi.
Population: About 79 million
Currency: Deutsche Mark
Main language: German
Full name: Federal Republic of Germany

Capital city: Berlin. This city was once divided by a high wall mounted with guns. Today, people can go wherever they like in the city.

The Brandenburg Gate, Berlin

Black Forest pinewoods

Landscape: There are many different kinds of scenery. The beautiful Rhine River Valley and the Black Forest are very famous. The Zugspitze (9,722 ft.) is the highest mountain. The longest river is the Elbe (724 mi.).

Neuschwanstein Castle, Bavaria

Industries

Chemicals
Vehicles
Engineering
Coal
Shipbuilding

Places to visit: There are historic cities and ancient castles in the regions of Bavaria and Saxony. In the north there are sandy beaches.

Norway

Norway lies along the coast of Scandinavia. Part of it is inside the Arctic Circle.

Oslo

Key facts

Size: 125,181 sq. mi.
Population: Over 4 million
Currency: Norwegian krone
Language: Norwegian

Capital city: Oslo. This is one of the world's largest cities, but only 500,000 people live here. You can visit many ancient Viking burial mounds and settlement sites in Norway.

Landscape: Norway has a long coastline, famous for its deep inlets called fjords. It also has over 150,000 islands. Mountains and moorland cover three-quarters of the country. Glittertind is the highest mountain (8,104 ft.). The longest river is the Glama (373 mi.).

A Norwegian fjord

Places to visit: The Norwegian mountains are famous for winter sports. There are about 10,000 ski jumps in the country, as well as lots of forest trails.

Industries

Oil
Paper-making
Timber
Fishing

Cross-country skiing in Norway

Sweden

Sweden is the largest Scandinavian country. It has a long coastline and many islands.

Stockholm

Key facts

Size: 173,731 sq. mi.
Population: Over 8 million
Currency: Swedish krona
Main language: Swedish

Capital city: Stockholm. The city is built on a string of islands. It is the home of the Royal Palace and many other historic buildings.

The Royal Palace

Landscape: Over half of Sweden is covered with forest. There are about 96,000 lakes in the south and centre of the country. Lapland (northern Sweden) is inside the Arctic Circle. Mount Kebnerkaise (6,926 ft.) is the highest peak in Sweden.

Places to visit: Sweden has thousands of islands which are ideal for boating and fishing. You can find out about Viking longboats in the Nordic Museum, Stockholm.

Industries

Timber
Vehicles
Electronics
Minerals
Chemicals

A Viking longboat

Denmark

Denmark is the smallest Scandinavian country. It is made up of a peninsula and about 400 islands.

Copenhagen

Key facts

Size: 16,629 sq. mi.
Population: Over 5 million
Currency: Danish krone
Main Language: Danish

Capital city: Copenhagen. This is a city with many old buildings, fountains and pretty squares. The well-known statue of the Little Mermaid sits on a rock in Copenhagen Harbor. The story of the mermaid was written by a famous Dane, Hans Christian Andersen.

The Little Mermaid

Landscape: Denmark has mainly low-lying countryside with forests and lakes. There are many beautiful sandy beaches and about 500 islands. Yding Skovhoj is the highest mountain (568 ft.). The longest river is the Guden (98 mi.).

Places to visit: Copenhagen has palaces, castles and a Viking museum. At Legoland™ Park everything is made of Lego™, including life-sized working trains and lots of miniature buildings.

Industries
Farming
Tourism
Textiles
Electronics
Oil

A Legoland™ train

The Netherlands

The Netherlands is one of the flattest European countries. Two-fifths is below sea level.

Amsterdam

Key facts

Size: 15,770 sq. mi.
Population: Over 15 million
Currency: Guilder
Main language: Dutch
Also called: Holland

Capital city: Amsterdam. This city is built on canals and is sometimes called "the Venice of the North." It has about a thousand bridges and many attractive seventeenth-century houses.

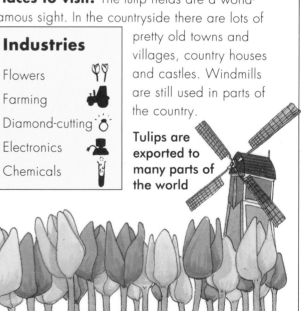
Amsterdam

Landscape: The Netherlands is very flat and is criss-crossed by rivers and canals. In the past, large areas of land were reclaimed from the sea. Sea-dams, called dykes, were built and the sea water was drained away. The highest point of land is only 1,056 ft.

Places to visit: The tulip fields are a world-famous sight. In the countryside there are lots of pretty old towns and villages, country houses and castles. Windmills are still used in parts of the country.

Industries
Flowers
Farming
Diamond-cutting
Electronics
Chemicals

Tulips are exported to many parts of the world

Italy

Italy is in southern Europe. The Mediterranean islands of Sicily and Sardinia are part of this country.

Rome

Sardinia

Sicily

Key facts

Size: 116,303 sq. mi.
Population: Over 57 million
Currency: Lira
Main language: Italian

Capital city: Rome. This was once the capital of the ancient Roman empire. It has lots of Roman remains, including the ruins of the Colosseum. Here, huge audiences watched as gladiators fought and Christians were thrown to the lions.

The Colosseum

In Rome there is a tiny separate country called Vatican City. This is the home of the Pope, the head of the Roman Catholic Church.

Landscape: There are spectacular mountains and beautiful lakes in the north. In central and southern regions you can see plains and smaller mountains. Italy has several live volcanoes, including Etna, Vesuvius and Stromboli. Mont Blanc is the highest mountain (15,771 ft.). The Po is the longest river (405 mi.).

Stromboli

Industries

Farming

Vehicles

Electronics

Fashion

Places to visit: Italy has many historic cities, such as Venice, which is built on a lagoon. The easiest way to travel around Venice is by gondola. Some of the world's greatest artists have lived in Italy. You can see their work in art galleries and museums.

A Venetian gondola

Greece

Greece juts out into the Mediterranean Sea. About one-fifth of the country is made up of small islands.

Athens

Key facts

Size: 50,949 sq. mi.
Population: Over 10 million
Currency: Drachma
Main language: Greek

Capital city: Athens. This is one of the world's oldest cities. On the top of the Acropolis ridge, you can see the ruins of the Parthenon. This Greek temple is 2,400 years old.

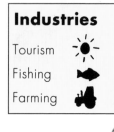

Landscape: Mainland Greece has plains and forests in the south and is mountainous in the north. Mount Olympus is the highest mountain (9,571 ft.). The Greek islands vary in size and landscape. Crete is the largest of these. The longest river in Greece is the Aliakmon (184 mi.).

Mount Olympus, legendary home of the ancient Greek gods

Industries

Tourism

Fishing

Farming

Places to visit: There are lots of ancient sites. Many of them are linked with stories from Greek mythology. For instance, the Palace of Knossos, on Crete, is the legendary home of the Minotaur monster.

The Minotaur

Poland

Poland is in Central Europe. It shares its borders with four other countries. Its coastline is on the Baltic Sea.

Key facts

Size: 120,725 sq. mi.
Population: Over 38 million
Currency: Zloty
Main language: Polish

Capital city: Warsaw. The old city of Warsaw was destroyed in World War Two. The "Old Town" area has been rebuilt in the style of the old buildings.

Warsaw "Old Town"

Landscape: There are many lakes and wooded hills in northern Poland, and beach resorts along the Baltic coast. Rysy Peak (8,212 ft.) is the highest point in the mountainous south. The longest river is the Vistula (664 mi.).

Industries

Farming
Coalmining
Shipbuilding
Timber

Places to visit: There are lots of museums and art galleries in Warsaw. There are several national parks where rare forest creatures live, such as lynxes and moose.

A rare lynx

Russia

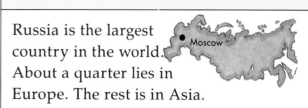

Russia is the largest country in the world. About a quarter lies in Europe. The rest is in Asia.

Key facts

Size: 6,592,812 sq. mi.
Population: About 150 million
Currency: Rouble
Main language: Russian

Capital city: Moscow. The famous Kremlin building is in the center of the city. It was once a fortress occupied by Tsars, Russian emperors, who ruled for centuries.

St. Basil's Cathedral, Moscow's famous landmark

Landscape: Russia is the world's largest country. It has some of the largest lakes and forests and longest rivers in the world. Mount Elbrus is the highest mountain (18,482 ft.). The longest river is the Volga (2,193 mi.).

Industries

Engineering
Farming
Oil
Minerals
Coal mining

Lake Baikal, is the world's deepest lake, at 6,365 ft.

Places to visit: Russia has many old cities, all with long and exciting histories. The world's longest railway, the Trans-Siberian, runs across the country from Moscow to Vladivostok.

The Trans-Siberian Railway

North America

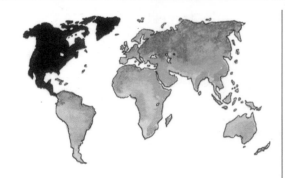

North America is the third largest continent in the world. It stretches from the frozen Arctic Circle down to the sunny Gulf of Mexico. It is so wide that there are eight different time zones.

Canada, the United States of America, Mexico, Greenland and the countries of Central America are all part of this continent.

The tropical south

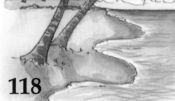

The islands of Hawaii, Bermuda and the West Indies lie off the mainland.

Key facts

Size: 9,035,000 sq. mi.
Largest country: Canada (second largest in the world) 3,851,787 sq. mi.
Longest river: Mississippi-Missouri (3,860 mi.)
Highest mountain: Mount McKinley (20,322 ft.)

Landscape

The North American landscape is very varied. There are huge forests, ice-covered wastelands, scorching deserts and wide grassy plains.

The Rocky Mountains

In the west, mountains run from Alaska down to Mexico. They are called the Cordillera, and include the Rocky Mountains. The Appalachian Mountains run down the eastern side.

A vast plain stretches about 2,983 mi. from the Gulf of Mexico to northern Canada. The Great Plains and the Mississippi-Missouri River are in this region. Much of the world's maize is grown here.

The most northern parts of the continent border the icy Arctic Ocean. This area is called tundra. Here, the land just beneath the surface is permanently frozen.

Weather

Temperatures vary from -164°F in an Arctic winter to 137°F in summer in Death Valley, California, one of the world's hottest places. Every year in North America, there are about 550 tornadoes, mostly in the central states of the U.S. Tornado winds can spin at up to 403 mph.

The frozen north

A tornado

 **Chemicals**  **Farming**  **Mining**  **Oil**

People

Long ago, North America was populated only by native American people, called Native American Indiains. Over the centuries, settlers came from Europe and slaves were brought from Africa. Now, most of the population is descended from these people.

For many centuries, the Canadian Arctic has been the home of the Inuit people.

Many people from the West Indies are descended from Africans captured and brought over to the country as slaves.

Economy

The continent of North America has many natural resources, such as oil, minerals and timber.

The U.S. is the world's richest country. It has many different industries.

Timber products, such as paper, come from the northern areas

Cities

The U.S. has many cities. New York City is the largest, with a population of over 17 million.

Although Canada is the biggest country in North America, it has a small population. Its major cities are all in the south of the country, where the climate is milder than the Arctic north.

The Statue of Liberty in New York City Harbor was the first sight many immigrants had of North America

Mexico City, in Mexico, is one of the most overcrowded cities in the world.

Map of North America

Approximate scale: 0 — 620 mi. — 1,240 mi.

Bering Strait · Arctic Ocean · Greenland (Denmark) · CANADA · Hudson Bay · Rocky Mountains · Great Lakes · Toronto · USA · Pacific Ocean · MEXICO · New York City · Atlantic Ocean · Mexico City · Gulf of Mexico · WEST INDIES · Hawaiian Islands · CENTRAL AMERICA · Carribean Sea

Map key

1 Bermuda
2 Bahamas
3 Cuba
4 Jamaica
5 Haiti
6 Dominican Republic
7 Puerto Rico

U.S.A.

The United States of America stretches from the Atlantic Ocean to the Pacific. It includes Alaska in the north and the Hawaiian Islands in the Pacific Ocean.

Washington D.C.

Key facts

Size: 3,618,766 sq. mi.
Population: Over 250 million
Currency: U.S. dollar
Main language: English

Capital city: Washington, D.C. This is the center of government. The President lives here in the White House.

The White House

The U.S. flag is called the "Stars and Stripes". It has thirteen red and white stripes which stand for the first thirteen states. The country now has fifty states, shown by the fifty stars on the flag.

Landscape: As well as mountain ranges, vast plains and deserts, there is the deep land gorge, the Grand Canyon, in Arizona. Mount McKinley is the highest point (20,322 ft.). The Mississippi-Missouri (3,860 mi.) is the longest river.

Grand Canyon

Places to visit: The U.S. has many historic sites, big cities and beach resorts. Famous places include Hollywood in California, Disney World™ in Florida, and many national parks.

Industries

Farming
Oil
Steel
Vehicles
Space

The famous Hollywood sign

Canada

Canada is the largest country in North America. Its northern part is inside the Arctic Circle.

Ottowa

Key facts

Size: 3,851,787 sq. mi.
Population: About 27 million
Currency: Canadian dollar
Main languages: English and French

Capital city: Ottowa. Canada is divided into ten provinces and two territories. Ottowa is in the province of Ontario.

The CN Tower, the world's tallest free-standing structure (1,814 ft. high), is in Toronto, the largest city in Canada.

CN Tower

Landscape: Nearly half of Canada is covered by forest. The Great Lakes, the world's largest group of freshwater lakes, are on the border with the U.S. The Rocky Mountains are in the west. In the center, there are vast plains, called prairies. The highest mountain is Mount Logan (19,525 ft.). The Mackenzie is the longest river (2,635 mi.).

The Rocky Mountains

A totem pole

Industries

Farming
Forestry
Vehicles

Places to visit: You can see ancient totem poles in Stanley Park, Vancouver. Canada has lots of national park areas, where bears and wolves live. The world-famous Niagara Falls is a spectacular sight.

Mexico

Mexico lies south of the U.S.A. and north of South America.

Mexico City

Key facts

Size: 692,102 sq. mi.
Population: Over 80 million
Currency: Peso
Main language: Spanish

Capital city: Mexico City. Almost one-fifth of the population lives here. There are modern buildings next to ancient Aztec ruins.

Mexico once belonged to Spain. You can still see many Spanish-style buildings and churches.

A Spanish-style church

Landscape: More than half the country is over 3,200 ft. high. Central Mexico is a plateau surrounded by volcanic mountains. There are also deserts and swamps. Mount Orizaba (18,702 ft.) is the highest mountain. The longest river is the Rio Grande (1,299 mi.), which flows along the U.S. border.

Industries

Coffee
Oil
Minerals
Crafts

Places to visit: Aztec, Mayan and Toltec people once ruled Mexico. You can still see the remains of cities and temples they built.

A Mayan temple

Jamaica

Jamaica is an island in the Caribbean Sea, south of Cuba.

Kingston

Key facts

Size: 4,244 sq. mi.
Population: Over 2 million
Currency: Jamaican dollar
Main language: English

Capital city: Kingston. Built by a deep, sheltered harbor, this city was once ruled by a pirate, Captain Morgan, and his Buccaneers.

Captain Morgan

Landscape: Jamaica is a tropical island with lush rainforests, pretty waterfalls and dazzling white beaches. It is actually the tip of an undersea mountain range. Blue Mountain Peak (7,401 ft.) is the highest mountain on the island.

Places to visit: As well as beaches, there are wildlife parks and bird sanctuaries where some of the world's most exotic birds can be seen. There are working sugar and banana plantations.

Industries

Tourism
Minerals
Farming

A Jamaican beach

South America

South America is the world's fourth largest continent. It stretches from the border of Central America to the tip of Chile.

There are 13 South American countries, each with its own distinctive type of landscape and culture.

For centuries the continent was populated only by native peoples. Europeans did not arrive until 1499. Now, many of the people are descended from these Spanish or Portuguese settlers.

Early settlers came from Europe

A Spanish-style church

Landscape

There are lots of different landscapes, including high mountains, hot and cold deserts, rainforests and plains.

The world's longest mountain range is the Andes, which runs all the way down the western side. Some of its mountains are live volcanoes. There are also regular earthquakes in this area.

Between the highland areas there are vast lowlands. Much of these areas are covered by dense rainforests. There are also grasslands, such as the Argentinian pampas.

There are some live volcanoes in the Andes Mountain Range

South America has many dense rainforests

People

Many large South American cities are on the eastern coast. Outside the cities, most people live on small farms, growing just enough food to feed themselves.

There are still a few Amerindians (native Americans) living in forest settlements deep in the Amazon River Basin. They hunt animals, gather fruit and grow crops to eat.

Largest country:
Brazil
(3,286,470 sq. mi.)

Smallest country:
French Guiana
(38,749 sq. mi.)

Highest mountain:
Mount Aconcagua
(22,836 ft.)
Longest river:
Amazon
(4,000 mi.)

Amazon butterflies

A jaguar

The Amazon

The Amazon River carries more fresh water than any other. It flows across South America from the Andes to the Atlantic and drains more than 2 million sq. mi. of land, much of it rainforest. It is one of the world's richest wildlife areas, with many extraordinary creatures such as hummingbirds, sloths, jaguars and piranha fish.

A hummingbird

Weather

In rainforest areas, it is warm and humid all the time and it rains almost daily.

The warmest part of South America is in northern Argentina. The coldest place is Tierra Del Fuego, which faces Antarctica at the southern tip of the continent.

The world's driest place is the Atacama Desert in Chile. Until 1971 it had not rained there for 400 years.

Industries

Coffee
Forestry
Cacao
Oil
Farming
Minerals

Map of South America

Approximate scale: 0 ____ 620 mi. ____ 1,240 mi.

Caracas
VENEZUELA
Orinoco River
COLOMBIA
2
3 4
1
PERU
EQUATOR
Amazon River
BRAZIL
Lima
La Paz
BOLIVIA
Brasiliá
Pacific Ocean
CHILE
6
Paraná River
São Paulo
Santiago
5
Buenos Aires
ARGENTINA
Atlantic Ocean
Falkland Islands (U.K.)
Tierra del Fuego
(Chile) (Argentina)

Map key

1 Equador
2 Guyana
3 Surinam
4 French Guiana
5 Uruguay
6 Paraguay

Brazil

Brazil covers almost half of South America. It is the fifth-largest country in the world.

Brasilia

Key facts

Size: 3,286,470 sq. mi.
Population: Over 150 million
Currency: Cruzeiro
Main language: Portuguese

Capital city: Brasilia. This city was begun in the 1950s. It is famous for its futuristic architecture.

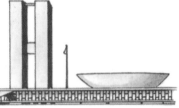

Brasilia's futuristic buildings

Landscape: Brazil has over 1 million sq. mi. of rainforest. The mighty Amazon River (4,000 mi.) runs through it, carrying more water than any other river in the world. Pica da Neblina (9,889 ft.) is the highest mountain in Brazil.

Flesh-eating piranha fish live in the Amazon River

Industries

Coffee
Sugar cane
Timber
Iron
Precious gems

Places to visit: The Amazon Rainforest has many thousands of animal and plant species. It is also the home of the Amazon Indians. Ecologists are trying to save the forest from destruction.

Rainforest birds

Argentina

Argentina lies to the east of the Andes Mountains, facing the Atlantic Ocean.

Buenos Aires

Key facts

Size: 1,068,296 sq. mi.
Population: Over 32 million
Currency: Austral
Main language: Spanish

Capital city: Buenos Aires. This is one of the largest cities in the southern half of the world. It is the birthplace of the famous tango dance.

Dancing the tango

Landscape: The scenery includes hot desert, the Andes Mountain Range and the cold wilderness of the Patagonia Desert in the south. Mount Aconcagua (22,836 ft.) is the highest point. The longest river is the Paraná (3,032 mi.).

Argentinian grassland, called pampas

Places to visit: There are historic cities, beach resorts and wildlife parks in Argentina. The Andes is home to the spectacular and rare bird, the condor.

Industries

Farming
Textiles
Steel
Chemicals

A condor

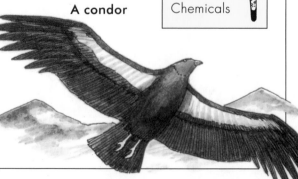

Peru

Peru is on the Pacific coast of South America. The Andes Mountains run down the center.

Key facts

Size: 496,222 sq. mi.
Population: Over 22 million
Currency: New Sol
Main languages: Spanish, Quechua

Capital city: Lima. This city was founded by the Spaniard, Francisco Pizarro, in 1535. He attacked and conquered Peru in the 1500s in search of its legendary treasure.

Francisco Pizarro

Landscape: Peru is a country of deserts, mountains and rainforests, some of it still unexplored. The source of the Amazon River is in the Peruvian Andes. The highest point is Mount Huascarán (22,206 ft.). The Ucayli is the longest river (910 mi.).

Industries

Farming
Coffee
Cotton
Fishing
Minerals

The Andes Mountains

Places to visit: Peru was once ruled by the Inca people. They built fabulous palaces, towers and temples covered in gold. You can visit the ruins of their cities, such as Cuzco and Machu Picchu.

Machu Picchu

Venezuela

Venezuela is on the north coast of South America. This is where Christopher Columbus first set foot on the American mainland.

Caracas

Key facts

Size: 352,142 sq. mi.
Population: Over 20 million
Currency: Bolívar
Main language: Spanish

Capital city: Caracas. The national hero, Simon Bolívar, is buried here. He helped to free Venezuela from the Spanish. Many buildings and streets are named after him.

Simon Bolívar

Landscape: There are lowland and highland areas. One of the lowland areas is a dense alligator-infested forest around the Orinoco River. Some of the highlands are still unexplored. Mount Bolívar is the highest point (16,428 ft.). The Orinoco (1,700 mi.) is the longest river.

Industries

Fruit
Coffee
Minerals
Tourism

The Venezuelan landscape

Places to visit: Venezuela has some of the most spectacular scenery in the world. the world's highest waterfall, Angel Falls (3,212 ft.) is in the Canaima National Park.

Angel Falls

Africa

Africa is the second largest continent in the world. It is only 8 mi. to the south of Europe, across the Strait of Gibraltar. A strip of land called the Isthmus of Suez separates the continent from Asia.

There are 670 million people in Africa, but they are spread thinly throughout more than 50 countries.

Large parts of Africa are

Nairobi, Kenya

uninhabited because the climate is harsh and the terrain makes travel difficult. There are mountains, rainforests, deserts and grassland, called savannah.

African desert

Key facts

Size: 11,684,158 sq. mi.
Population: 670 million
Largest country: Sudan
Smallest country: Seychelles
Highest mountain: Mount Kilimanjaro (19,341ft.)
Longest river: Nile (4,145 mi.)

Mount Kilimanjaro

Landscape

Much of Africa is on a high plateau. Around this high, flat tableland there are narrow coastal plains. The highest mountains are in East Africa.

The Sahara Desert crosses the northern part of Africa. It is the biggest desert in the world, spreading out over a huge area almost as large as the U.S.A! Some parts of it are sandy, but much of it is rocky wasteland.

In central Africa, there are dense tropical rainforests. In southern Africa there are savannah and desert areas.

The Nile River is the longest river in the world. It flows north to the Mediterranean Sea.

The Nile River

Animals

Africa is very rich in wildlife. Many of the large mammals live on the wide grassy plains of the savannah.

Some species of animals are in danger of dying out. To save them, large areas have been made into reserves and national parks, where hunting is illegal.

African savannah

Jambo!
Swahili

Salam walaykoom!
Moroccan

Ekale!
Yaruba

Weather

The Equator crosses Africa. Here there are hot, humid rainforests where it rains almost every day.

African rainforest

People

In the north, many people speak Arabic and follow the Muslim religion.

Pygmy people live in the rainforests of Congo and Zaïre.

In South Africa, black people make up two-thirds of the population. For many years they have had few rights. This is now beginning to change.

Economy

Many Africans are farmers. They work on the land growing crops such as peanuts and cocoa beans (used for making chocolate).

A major industry is mining. Africa is rich in minerals such as gold, silver, tin and copper. It has large stores of oil and natural gas.

A farmer harvesting his crop

Map key

1	Algeria	28	Malawi
2	Angola	29	Mali
3	Benin	30	Mauritania
4	Botswana	31	Mauritius
5	Burkina Faso	32	Morocco
6	Burundi	33	Mozambique
7	Cameroon	34	Namibia
8	Cape Verde	35	Niger
9	Central African Republic	36	Nigeria
10	Chad	37	Rwanda
11	Comoros	38	São Tomé & Principe
12	Congo	39	Senegal
13	Djibouti	40	Seychelles
14	Egypt	41	Sierra Leone
15	Equatorial Guinea	42	Somali Republic
16	Ethiopia	43	South Africa
17	Gabon	44	Sudan
18	Gambia	45	Swaziland
19	Ghana	46	Tanzania
20	Guinea	47	Togo
21	Guinea-Bissau	48	Tunisia
22	Ivory Coast	49	Uganda
23	Kenya	50	Western Sahara
24	Lesotho	51	Zaire
25	Liberia	52	Zambia
26	Libya	53	Zimbabwe
27	Madagascar		

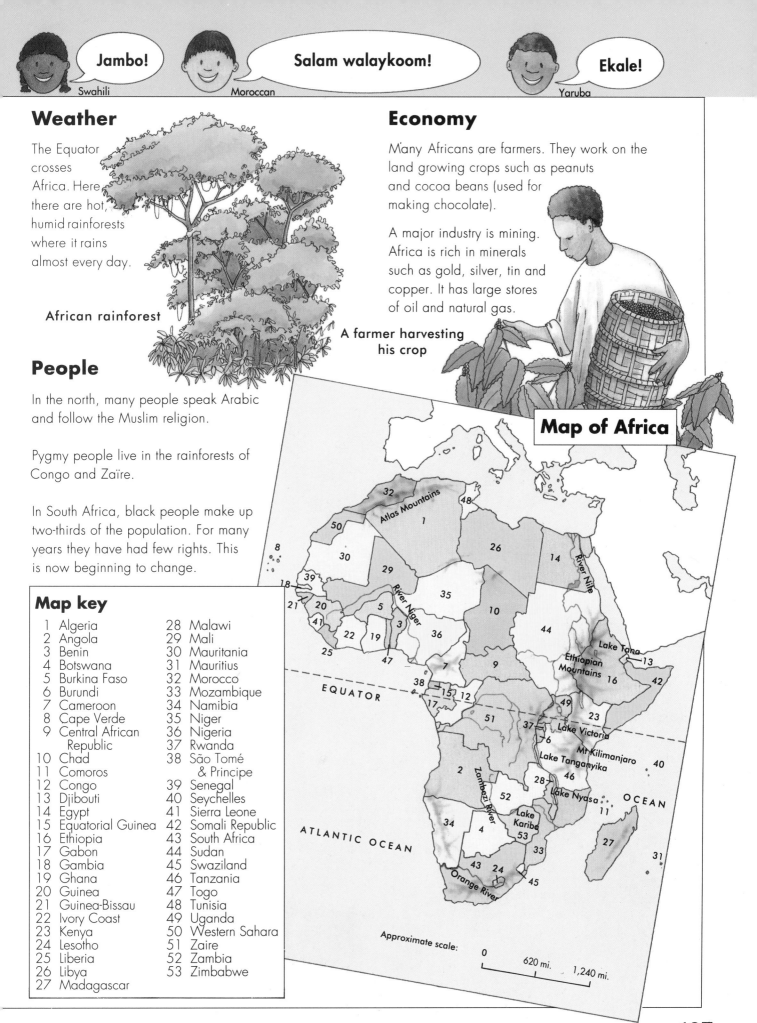

Map of Africa

Atlas Mountains
River Nile
River Niger
EQUATOR
Lake Tana
Ethiopian Mountains
Lake Victoria
Mt Kilimanjaro
Lake Tanganyika
Lake Nyasa
Lake Kariba
Zambezi River
Orange River
ATLANTIC OCEAN
OCEAN

Approximate scale:
0   620 mi.   1,240 mi.

127

South Africa

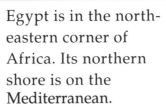

South Africa is at the southernmost tip of the African continent.

Key facts
Size: 471,442 sq. mi.
Population: Over 40 million
Currency: Rand
Main languages: English, Afrikaans.

Capital cities: South Africa has three capital cities called Pretoria, Bloemfontein and Cape Town. Each plays a different part in the government of the country.

Table Mountain, near Cape Town

Landscape: South Africa has a huge high plateau bordered by mountains. On the plateau there are wide grassy plains called the "veld." The long coastline has lots of beautiful beaches. The highest point is Champagne Castle in the Drakensberg (11,074 ft.). The Orange River (1,305 mi.) is the longest river.

Industries

Mining
Precious gems
Farming

South Africa is famous for its diamond mines

Places to visit: There are several famous wildlife reserves. You can see eagles, elephants, giraffes, lions and tigers living in their natural habitat.

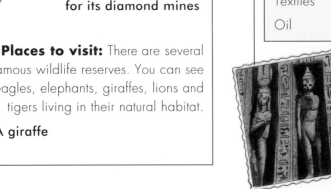

A giraffe

Egypt

Egypt is in the north-eastern corner of Africa. Its northern shore is on the Mediterranean.

Key facts
Size: 386,659 sq. mi.
Population: Over 55 million
Currency: Egyptian pound
Main language: Arabic

Capital city: Cairo. This is a center of historic monuments and unique historical sites.

The Ancient Egyptian civilization began about 5,000 years ago. The Pyramids at Giza were built as tombs for the Pharoahs, the kings who ruled at that time.

The pyramids and Sphinx at Giza, just outside Cairo

Landscape:
The country is divided by the great Nile River. A belt of green fertile land runs along the river and spreads out around its delta (river mouth). The rest of Egypt is sandy desert. The highest mountain is Jabal Katrinah (8,652 ft.). The Nile River is the world's longest river (4,000 mi.).

Farming the Nile delta

Industries
Tourism
Textiles
Oil

Places to visit: Some pharoahs were buried in the Valley of the Kings. You can see their tomb treasures on display. There are huge temples at Luxor and Abu Simbel. Around the Red Sea there are beaches and spectacular coral reefs.

The great temple of Abu Simbel

Nigeria

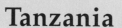

Nigeria's coast is on the Gulf of Guinea in western Africa.

Key facts

Size: 356,667 sq. mi.
Population: Over 88 million
Currency: Naira
Main language: The official language is English but there are over 250 local languages

Capital city: In 1991 Abuja became the new capital city, in place of Lagos.

Many people live in villages. The main groups of people are the Hausa, Ibo and Yoruba.

A village market

Landscape: There are lagoons, beaches and mangrove swamps along the coast. Inland, there are rainforests where the trees can grow as high as 100 ft. An area of grassland with scattered trees, called the savannah, lies in the south.

Coastal mangrove swamp

Industries

Oil
Cacao
Palm oil
Minerals

Places to visit: Many ancient cultures flourished in Nigeria. There are several historic cities, such as Kano, famous for its festival of horsemanship. There are wildlife parks and spectacular scenery.

A Yoruba festival mask and drummer

Tanzania

Tanzania lies in eastern Africa on the Indian Ocean. It includes the islands of Zanzibar and Pemba.

Key facts

Size: 364,896 sq. mi.
Population: About 25 million
Currency: Tanzanian shilling
Main languages: English, Swahili

Capital city: Dodoma. Dar es Salaam is the largest city and main port.

There are about 120 groups of people in Tanzania including the wandering Masai, the tallest people in the world.

Masai women

Landscape: Most of Tanzania consists of a high plateau. Savannah and bush cover about half the country. There are huge inland lakes. Mount Kilimanjaro (19,341 ft.), in Nigeria, is the highest mountain in Africa. The longest river is the Rufiji.

An inland lake

Industries

Farming
Cotton
Coffee
Minerals

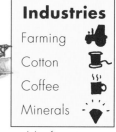

Places to visit: Some of the world's finest wildlife parks are here, including the Serengeti Plain and the Ngorongoro volcano.

Lake Manyara is famous for its tree-climbing lions

Shalom!
Hebrew

A-salam alekum!
Dhivehi (Maldives)

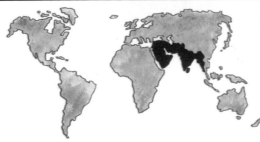

This area stretches about 3,107 mi. from the Mediterranean Sea to the Bay of Bengal. It includes Middle Eastern countries such as Saudi Arabia and the south Asian countries of Pakistan, Afghanistan, India and Bangladesh. The island of Sri Lanka and the mountainous countries of Bhutan and Nepal are also in this vast area.

The landscape varies from barren desert to the Himalayas, the highest mountains in the world.

Middle Eastern desert

The mountains of Nepal

Key facts

Size: 4,420,845 sq. mi.
Population: About 1330 million
Longest river: Ganges (2,900 mi.)
Highest mountain: Mount Everest (29,030 ft.)
Largest country: India (1,269,338 sq. mi.)
Smallest country: Maldives (115 sq. mi.)

Landscape

The landscape of Western and Southern Asia includes high mountains, wide plains, deserts and rainforests.

Mountains run all the way from Turkey to Afghanistan and dry, scrubby grassland stretches from Pakistan to Syria.

Desert covers most of Saudi Arabia and the surrounding lands.

Weather

The mountainous northern areas of the Middle East have hot summers and freezing winters. Farther south, it is hot all year round.

In India and Bangladesh, the farmers rely on the monsoon for their crops to grow. The monsoon is a season of heavy rain that falls between June and October.

Middle Eastern desert and mountains in Afghanistan

Monsoon rainfall in Southern Asia

Marhabah assalamu aleikum!
Arabic

Namaste!
Hindi

Min ga la baa!
Burmese

People

There are many different cultures in this area. Here are some examples:

In the Middle East, many people follow the Muslim faith. They pray every day facing the Holy City of Mecca, the center of their religion.

Many Indians are Hindus. They worship several gods, the chief of which is called Brahman. Some Indians follow the Sikh faith. Many Sikhs live in the Punjab region.

To Hindus, cows are sacred animals and are allowed to graze wherever they like

Economy

The countries around the Persian Gulf, in the Middle East, have vast oil reserves. They depend on the money they make from selling this oil around the world.

Throughout Southern Asia many different crops are grown, including wheat, millet, rice and cotton. India and Sri Lanka are among the world's biggest tea producers.

Tea picking

Main industries

Oil	Farming
Mining	Textiles

Map of Western & Southern Asia

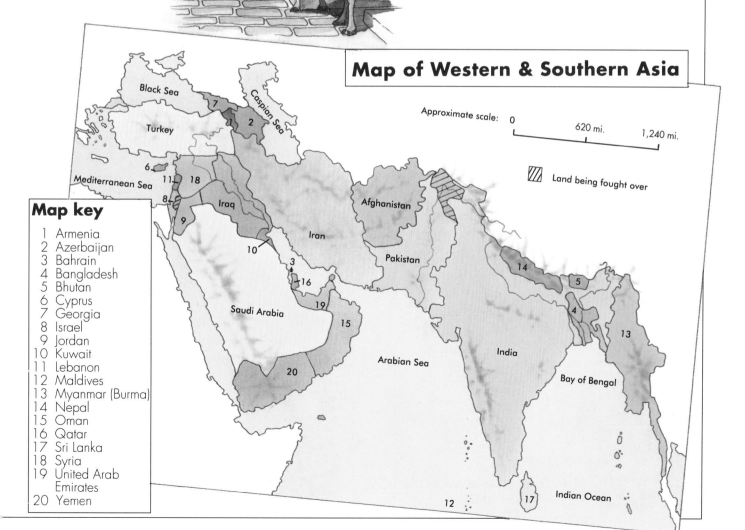

Approximate scale: 0 — 620 mi. — 1,240 mi.

▨ Land being fought over

Black Sea
Caspian Sea
Turkey
Mediterranean Sea
Iraq
Iran
Afghanistan
Pakistan
Saudi Arabia
India
Arabian Sea
Bay of Bengal
Indian Ocean

Map key

1. Armenia
2. Azerbaijan
3. Bahrain
4. Bangladesh
5. Bhutan
6. Cyprus
7. Georgia
8. Israel
9. Jordan
10. Kuwait
11. Lebanon
12. Maldives
13. Myanmar (Burma)
14. Nepal
15. Oman
16. Qatar
17. Sri Lanka
18. Syria
19. United Arab Emirates
20. Yemen

Israel

Israel is on the Mediterranean coast. The modern country of Israel was founded in 1948.

Jerusalem

Key facts

Size: 80,220 sq. mi.
Population: About 5 million
Currency: Shekel
Main languages: Hebrew, Arabic

Capital city: Jerusalem. This ancient holy city is about 4,000 years old. It is a center of Judaism, Christianity and Islam. There are many important historic sites from the Bible and the Islamic holy book, the Koran.

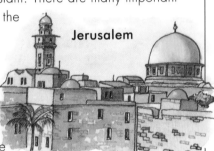
Jerusalem

Landscape: The hills of Galilea are in the north of Israel, and there is desert in the south. In between, there are fertile plains. The longest river is the Jordan (659 mi.), which flows into the Dead Sea. This sea is so salty that if you swim in it you cannot sink. Mount Meiron (3,963 ft.) is the highest point.

The Dead Sea

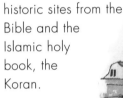

Places to visit: The history of this area goes back to about 2,000 B.C. There are many religious sites including the Wailing Wall, the Church of the Holy Sepulchre, the Mount of Olives and the Dome of the Rock. The town of Beersheba stands on the spot where Abraham is supposed to have pitched his tent 3,800 years ago.

Industries
Engineering
Electronics
Chemicals
Textiles
Fruit

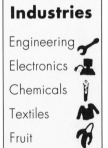

The Tomb of Absalom on the Mount of Olives

Saudi Arabia

Saudi Arabia covers about four-fifths of the Arabian peninsula. It is more than four times as big as France.

Riyadh

Key facts

Size: 829,995 sq. mi.
Population: Over 14 million
Currency: Saudi Riyal
Main language: Arabic

Capital city: Riyadh. This modern city is built on an ancient site. It is the home of the ruling Royal Family.

The Bedouin people wander the desert in search of grazing for their animals

Landscape:
Much of the country is barren desert scattered with oases. The Rub Al-Khali ("Empty Quarter"), in the south, is the largest sand desert in the world. The highest point is in the Asir Range (10,279 ft.). There are no rivers in Saudi Arabia!

Giant sand dunes in the "Empty Quarter"

Places to visit: Only Muslims are allowed to visit the sacred cities of Mecca and Medina. The Prophet Muhammad was born in Mecca and Muslims pray toward it, wherever they are in the world. Other ancient sites include camel markets, potteries and salt mines dating back 5,000 years.

Industries
Oil
Natural gas
Farming

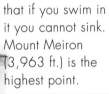

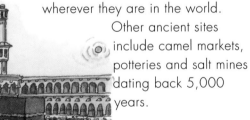

The sacred city of Mecca

Iran

Iran is in Western Asia, east of the Mediterranean Sea. It borders the Caspian Sea.

Key facts

Size: 636,293 sq. mi.
Population: About 57 million
Currency: Rial
Main language: Persian (Farsi)

Capital city: Tehran. The old city gates are in the old part of Tehran. It has one of the world's largest bazaars, where you can buy everything from carpets to silver and exotic spices.

A holy mosque

Landscape: Most of the cities are near the Caspian Sea, where the land is fertile. The rest of Iran is barren desert where much of Iran's oil is found. There are mountains in the western part of the country. The highest point is Mount Demavend (18,387 ft.).

Oil wells in the desert

Industries
Oil
Farming
Crafts

Places to visit: Iran was once called Persia. It was on the Silk Route, an important trail for merchants bringing silk and spices from the east. There are many ancient cities, museums and remains of the Roman and Persian Empires.

The Bakhtiari people spend the summer in the Zagros Mountains and the winter in the lowland areas of Iran

India

India is in Southern Asia between the Arabian Sea and the Bay of Bengal.

Key facts

Size: 1,269,338 sq. mi.
Population: Over 870 million
Currency: Rupee
Main languages: Hindi, English

Capital city: New Delhi. This modern city stands beside Old Delhi, where there are many ancient streets, temples, mosques and bazaars. The biggest city in India is Calcutta. Nine million people live there.

Old Delhi

India is the seventh largest country in the world, with the second biggest population after China.

Landscape: India is separated from the rest of Asia by the Himalayan mountain range in the north. In the north, many people live on the huge river plains of the Ganges and the Brahmaputra. Kanchenjunga (28,210 ft.) is the world's second highest mountain. The Brahmaputra (1,802 mi.) is the longest river.

Ganges

Industries
Farming
Chemicals
Electronics
Oil

Places to visit: There are many temples and palaces from the days when maharajahs ruled India. The most famous monument is the Taj Mahal.

The Taj Mahal

Ni hao! Cantonese

Haere-nai! Maori

This vast area includes China and its neighboring countries. Over one-fifth of the world's population lives in China. Asian Russia (to the east of the Ural Mountains) is in this region.

Malaysia and Indonesia (a group of thousands of islands) stretch down towards Australasia. This region includes Australia, the world's smallest continent, and New Zealand.

Chinese junks in the Pacific

Key facts about Northern & Eastern Asia

Size: About 12,399,601 sq. mi.
Largest country: Russia (about 4,835,516 sq. mi. in Asia)
Longest river: Chang (Yangtze) (3,915 mi.)
Highest mountain: Mount Everest (29,030 ft.)

Key facts about Australasia

Size: About 3,243,240 sq. mi.
Largest country: Australia (2,967,892 sq. mi.)
Longest river: Murray (1,609 mi.)
Highest mountain: Mount Wilhelm (14,794 ft.)

Landscape

Asian Russia has vast plains, with mountains in the far east and south. There is tundra in the Himalayas, with grassland and desert in central China.

Tropical rainforest stretches from southern China down through Malaysia, Indonesia and New Guinea. Some of this forest is still unexplored.

An erupting volcano

Part of this area is in the "Pacific Ring of Fire." It is called this because it has so many active volcanoes.

Much of Australia is dry grassland, with few trees. Australians call this the "outback" or "bush." There are also low mountain ranges, rainforests and deserts.

Weather

In the Himalayan mountains it is cold all year round. Farther south the weather is warm all the time. The monsoon season brings heavy rainfall to South-East Asia. Hurricanes (also called typhoons) often blow in this area. They are giant, spinning masses of wind and rain, sometimes stretching as wide as 300mi. across.

Hurricanes can blow at over 90 mph.

Selamat pagi!
Malaysian

Ohayo gozaimasu!
Japanese

G'day!
Australian

Economy

Eastern Asia is mainly farmland. Much of the world's rice is grown here. Rubber is also exported from here, all around the world. The rubber is made from milky sap, called latex, drained from trees.

Australia and New Zealand are important sheep-farming centers. In both countries, there are far more sheep than people. The sheep's wool and meat are exported to countries around the world.

Japan is one of the most powerful industrial countries in the world. It is famous for its electronic goods, such as computers and music systems. Japanese cars are exported all around the world.

Main industries

Farming

Mining

Oil

Shipbuilding

Forestry

Sheep

Map key

1 Brunei
2 Cambodia
3 Hong Kong
4 Kyrgyzstan
5 Laos
6 Macao
7 North Korea
8 Papua New Guinea
9 Singapore
10 South Korea
11 Taiwan
12 Tajikistan
13 Thailand
14 Turkmenistan
15 Uzbekistan
16 Vietnam

Map of Northern & Eastern Asia & Australasia

Japan

Japan is a chain of islands off the east coast of Asia, in the Pacific Ocean.

●Tokyo

Key facts

Size: 145,833 sq. mi.
Population: About 125 million
Currency: Yen
Main language: Japanese

Capital city: Tokyo is one of the world's most crowded cities. The Imperial Palace, where the present Emperor still lives, is here.

The Imperial Palace

Japan has many islands. The four main ones are called Kyushu, Shikoku, Honshu and Hokkaido.

Landscape:

Two-thirds of Japan is mountainous. The only flat land is along the coast. There are over 200 volcanoes, half of them active. The highest point in Japan is Mount Fuji (12,389 ft.). The Shinano-gawa (228 mi.) is the longest river.

Mount Fuji

Industries

Vehicles
Electronics
Farming
Shipbuilding

Places to visit: There are many temples dedicated to the god Buddha, historic sites and ancient palaces. If you visit Japan you are likely to see traditional crafts, and rituals such as the tea ceremony.

A Japanese temple

China

China is in Eastern Asia. It is nearly as big as the whole of Europe.

●Beijing

Key facts

Size: 3,705,386 sq. mi.
Population: Over 1,150 million (about one-fifth of the world's people)
Currency: Yuan
Main language: Mandarin Chinese

Capital city: Beijing. There are beautiful palaces and gardens to see. The Forbidden City is in the middle of Beijing. This was once the home of the Chinese emperors.

The Forbidden City

Landscape: There is a high plateau in the west, with flat lands in the east and several very long rivers. Mountains take up about one-third of the country. Mount Everest (29,030 ft.), on the border of China and Nepal, is the world's highest mountain. The Chang (3,436 mi.) is the longest river.

Mount Everest

Places to visit: The Great Wall of China runs from east to west for about 3,977 mi. It is the only structure on Earth visible from the Moon. The ancient tomb of emperor Quin Shihuangdi is at Xi'an. It was guarded by thousands of life-sized clay warriors, called the "terracotta army."

Industries

Farming
Minerals
Chemicals

The Great Wall of China

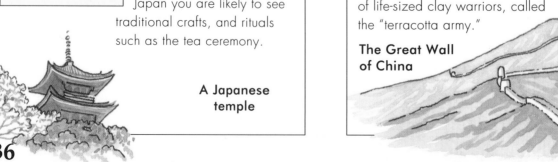

New Zealand

Wellington

New Zealand is in the Pacific. It is made up of two main islands, North Island and South Island.

Key facts

Size: 103,736 sq. mi.
Population: Over 3 million
Currency: New Zealand dollar
Main languages: English, Maori

Capital city: Wellington. Most people live in this city and the surrounding area. Wellington has a magnificent harbor and many old buildings.

Landscape: Much of the land is mountainous, with rivers and plains. In parts of North Island there are volcanoes, hot water geysers and pools of boiling mud. The highest point is Mount Cook (12,350 ft.). The Waikato (264 mi.) is the longest river.

Industries

Minerals

Farming

Wool

A geyser spouting hot water

Places to visit: There is lots of spectacular scenery, including rainforests and glaciers. The Maoris were the first settlers in this country. Rotorua is the center of Maori culture. Many kinds of animals and birds, such as the kiwi, are found only in New Zealand.

Maori dancers

Australia

Canberra

Australia lies 935 mi. north-west of New Zealand. It is the world's largest island.

Key facts

Size: 2,967,892 sq. mi.
Population: Over 17 million
Currency: Australian dollar
Main language: English

Capital city: Canberra. Most of the population lives along the eastern and south-eastern coastline. Australia is made up of six states and two territories, each with its own capital.

Sydney Opera House

Landscape: In the middle of Australia, there are several large deserts and dry grasslands. The Great Barrier Reef stretches 1,250 mi. along the north-east coast. The highest point in Australia is Mount Kosciusko (7,317 ft.). The Murray (1,609 mi.) is the longest river.

Ayers Rock, a famous landmark near Alice Springs

Industries

Farming

Minerals

Iron

Engineering

Places to visit: The original settlers in Australia were the Aborigines. Some of their cave paintings and historic sites date back to prehistoric times. There are wildlife parks where you can see koalas, kangaroos and other animals found only in Australia. The beaches are world-famous.

Sources of power

Before engines were invented nature was the only source of power available. Animals pulled carts, and the wind and running water moved windmills and water wheels. Water, wind and animal power are still important today.

However, engines are an important source of power. Cars, trucks, trains, aircraft and ships all have their own special engines to power them along.

Over 2,000 years ago the Ancient Greeks were using **water wheels** for grinding flour. Water was the main source of power for industry until steam engines were invented.

The weight of water falling into the buckets turned the wheel.

A Watt engine of the 1780s

Piston

The first **steam machine** was made before A.D. 100 by a Greek engineer, called Hero. It spun around as steam shot out of the pipes.

A **turbine** spins very fast when water flows through it. The turbine was invented in 1827. It soon replaced the water wheel.

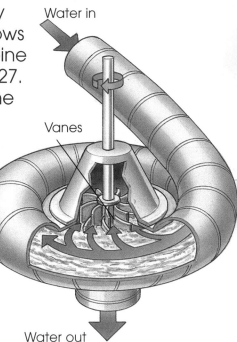

Water in

Vanes

Water pours into the turbine through a narrow pipe. It pushes the vanes round.

Water out

Windmills were first used around 650. They turned huge millstones which ground grain to make flour. They also pumped water and worked machinery.

In 1776 James Watt built a **steam engine** for pumping water out of coal and tin mines. Steam from boiling water moved a piston in and out. The moving piston worked the water pump.

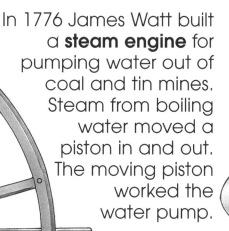

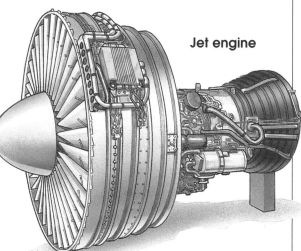

Jet engine

In 1939 the first aircraft with a **jet engine** took off. It was called the Heinkel He 178. Jet engines meant that aircraft could fly much faster than before.

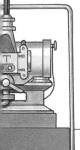

The sort of engine used in most modern cars is called an **internal combustion engine**. The first of these engines was built in 1860.

An internal combustion engine has cylinders and pistons like a steam engine. The first one used gas for fuel.

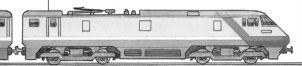

The wheel was one of the most important inventions in history. Think how difficult it would be to get around without it. Cars, bicycles, trains and carts use wheels.

For thousands of years carriages and carts were pulled by horses. But as soon as engines were invented people began making powered vehicles.

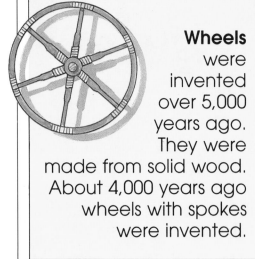

Wheels were invented over 5,000 years ago. They were made from solid wood. About 4,000 years ago wheels with spokes were invented.

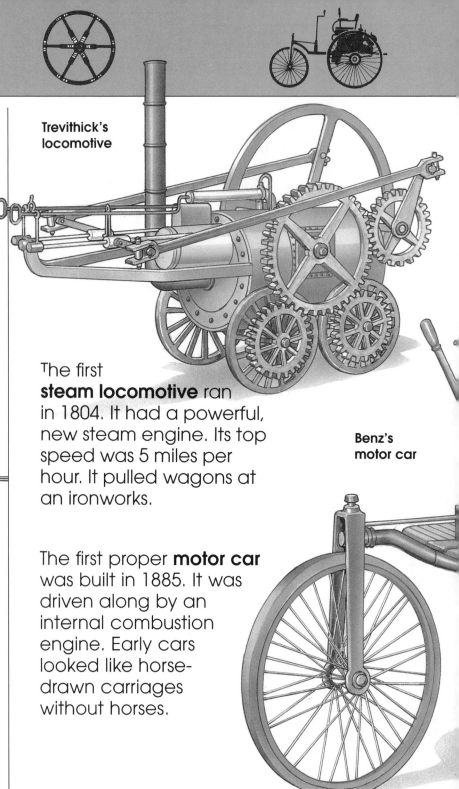

Trevithick's locomotive

The first **steam locomotive** ran in 1804. It had a powerful, new steam engine. Its top speed was 5 miles per hour. It pulled wagons at an ironworks.

The first proper **motor car** was built in 1885. It was driven along by an internal combustion engine. Early cars looked like horse-drawn carriages without horses.

Benz's motor car

The first **electric locomotive** was demonstrated in 1879 in Berlin.

The pedal **bicycle** was invented in 1839 by a Scottish blacksmith, called Kirkpatrick Macmillan. He only built one machine, which he rode himself.

To make the bicycle go, the rider pushed the pedals backward and forward.

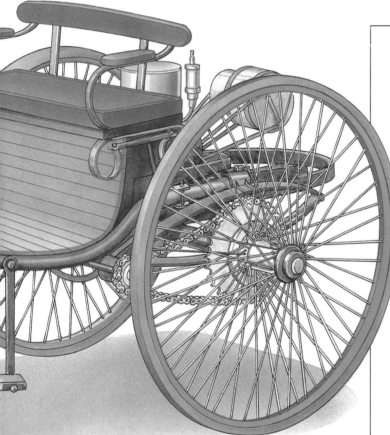

The first **motorcycle** was simply a bicycle fitted with a steam engine. It was built in 1868. The engine was under the saddle.

Steam engines powered tractors, trucks and buses. The first **steam vehicle** was designed to pull military cannons.

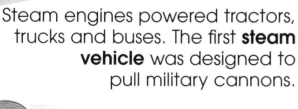

Cugnot built his steam tractor in 1769 or 1770. It was slow and quickly ran out of steam.

Ships and boats are very old inventions. Archaeologists think that people first made journeys in small boats 50,000 years ago. The boats were very simple canoes carved from tree trunks.

A triangular sail, called a **lateen sail,** was invented around 300 B.C. Boats with lateen sails could sail where their crews wanted them to.

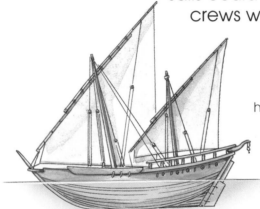

A type of boat called a dhow has a lateen sail.

In the 1400s **full rigging** was developed. Full-rigged ships had two or three masts with square and triangular sails.

Ships and boats are not only used for transporting people, but for trade, too. Today, most of the goods traded between different countries are sent by ship.

In the 1400s and 1500s European explorers, such as Christopher Columbus, sailed small full-rigged ships across the oceans.

Archaeologists don't really know when **sailboats** were invented. However, the Ancient Egyptians sailed boats made of reeds along the Nile River over 5,000 years ago.

These reed boats had square sails.

Soon after small portable steam engines were invented engineers built **steam-powered boats**. The *Charlotte Dundas* was built in 1801.

The engine turned large paddle wheels which pushed the boat through the water.

For thousands of years sailors steered using large oars attached to the side of their ship. The **rudder** was invented in China around 700.

Most modern ships are pushed along by a **propeller**. It was patented in 1836 and soon replaced paddle wheels.

A hydrofoil has wings which lift it out of the water. This means it can go much faster than ordinary boats.

Forlanini hydrofoil

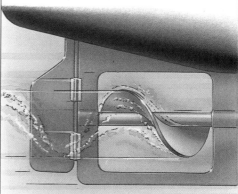

The idea for the **hydrofoil** was thought of in 1881. However, the first hydrofoil was not tested until 1905.

A **Hovercraft** is half boat, half airplane. It skims across sea or land on a cushion of air. The first practical Hovercraft was launched in 1959.

Flying machines

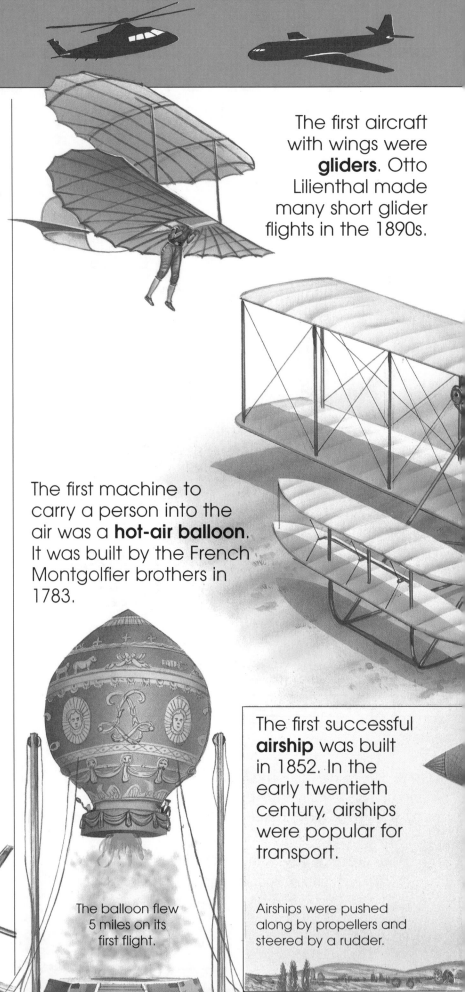

People dreamed of flying like birds for thousands of years before flying machines were made. Many people tried to copy the way birds flew. They tied wings to their arms, but with little success.

Today, there are many different types of aircraft. Every day, millions of people travel around the world in airliners and private aircraft. War planes include small fighters, bombers and huge transport planes.

The first aircraft with wings were **gliders**. Otto Lilienthal made many short glider flights in the 1890s.

The first machine to carry a person into the air was a **hot-air balloon**. It was built by the French Montgolfier brothers in 1783.

The balloon flew 5 miles on its first flight.

The first successful **airship** was built in 1852. In the early twentieth century, airships were popular for transport.

Airships were pushed along by propellers and steered by a rudder.

144

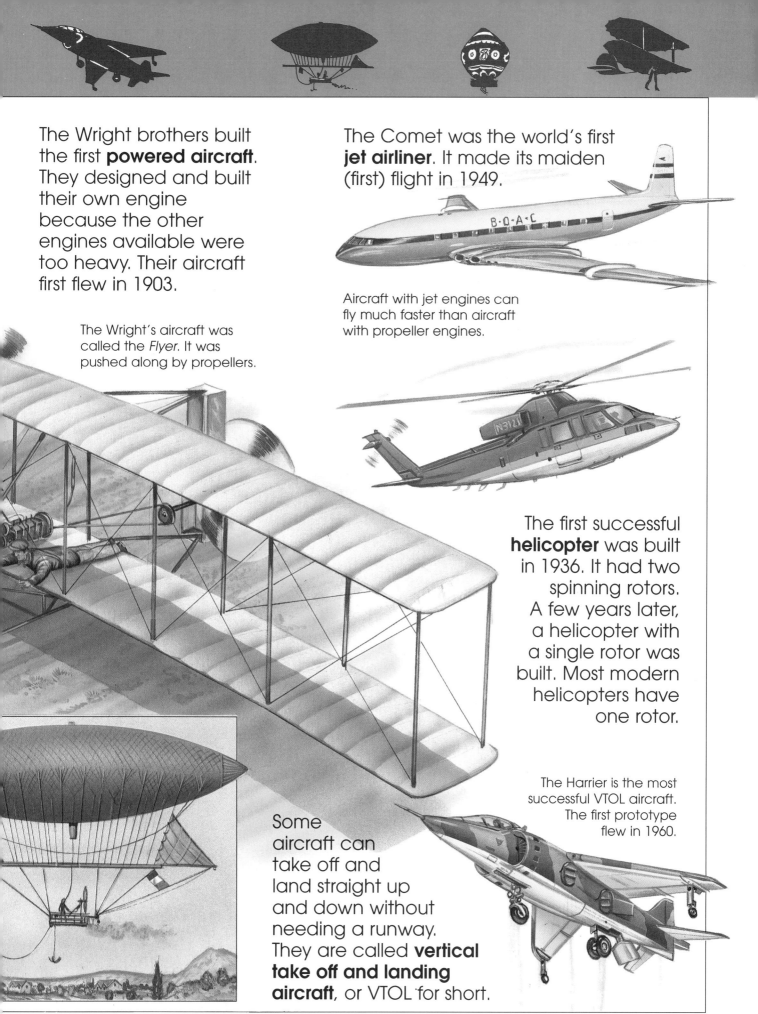

The Wright brothers built the first **powered aircraft**. They designed and built their own engine because the other engines available were too heavy. Their aircraft first flew in 1903.

The Wright's aircraft was called the *Flyer*. It was pushed along by propellers.

The Comet was the world's first **jet airliner**. It made its maiden (first) flight in 1949.

B·O·A·C

Aircraft with jet engines can fly much faster than aircraft with propeller engines.

N3121

The first successful **helicopter** was built in 1936. It had two spinning rotors. A few years later, a helicopter with a single rotor was built. Most modern helicopters have one rotor.

The Harrier is the most successful VTOL aircraft. The first prototype flew in 1960.

Some aircraft can take off and land straight up and down without needing a runway. They are called **vertical take off and landing aircraft**, or VTOL for short.

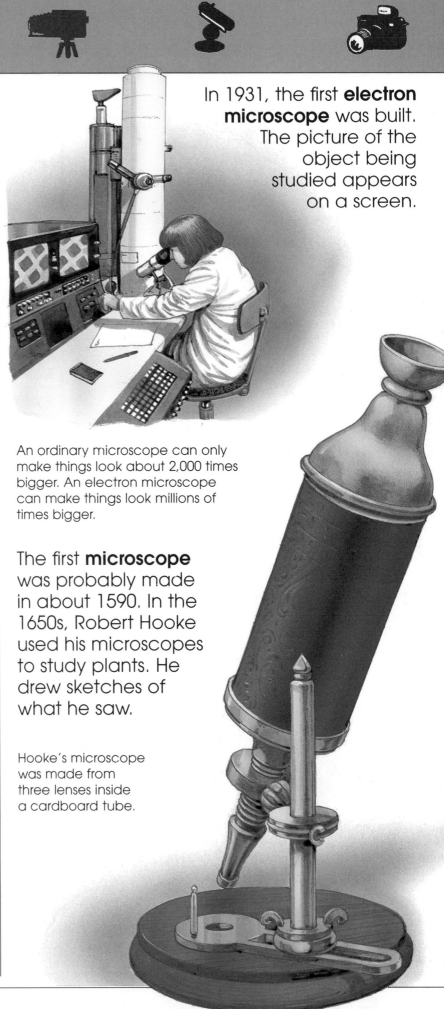

Five hundred years ago people could see only what was visible with their own eyes. Nobody knew how their bodies worked or what was out in space.

When the microscope and the telescope were invented, scientists and astronomers began to discover microscopic cells and millions of new stars.

In 1931, the first **electron microscope** was built. The picture of the object being studied appears on a screen.

An ordinary microscope can only make things look about 2,000 times bigger. An electron microscope can make things look millions of times bigger.

The first **microscope** was probably made in about 1590. In the 1650s, Robert Hooke used his microscopes to study plants. He drew sketches of what he saw.

Hooke's microscope was made from three lenses inside a cardboard tube.

The first **telescope** was probably made in 1608. The next year Galileo Galilei built his own telescope and used it to study the stars.

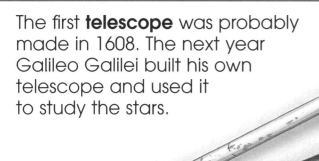

Using his telescopes, Galileo discovered that the Moon's surface is covered in craters.

A **reflecting telescope** uses mirrors instead of lenses. It was first made in 1668. Most telescopes used by astronomers are reflecting telescopes.

Isaac Newton's reflecting telescope

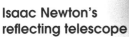

Radio telescopes collect radio waves coming from outer space.

Radio waves from space were first detected in 1931.

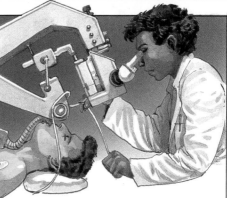

An **endoscope** is a long tube for seeing inside the human body. The first flexible one was built in 1956.

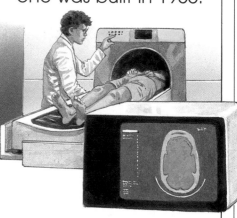

The first **medical scanner** was built in 1971 for looking inside the brain. Scanners for looking at the whole body soon followed.

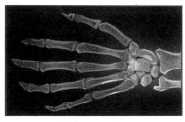

X-rays were discovered in 1895 by Wilhelm Röntgen. They were soon being used to take pictures of human bones.

The first clothes worn by human beings were made from animal skins and fur. Later, people learned to make cloth from other natural materials, such as plants, and still later, from artificial fibers.

Most types of cloth are made on a loom. The loom weaves threads together. Modern looms work automatically. Some weaving is still done on traditional hand looms.

Some materials, such as cotton and wool, have to be spun before they are woven. Spinning makes short fibers into long thread.

People started to spin wool and cotton fibers into thread many thousands of years ago. The first **spinning machine** was like a long spinning top.

The **spinning wheel** was probably invented in India. People started using it in Europe around the year 1300.

A spinning wheel spins and collects thread at the same time.

Around 1767 James Hargreaves invented a machine that he called the **spinning jenny**. It spun thread automatically and made spinning much quicker.

The **loom** appeared around 5000 B.C. The first looms were very simple.

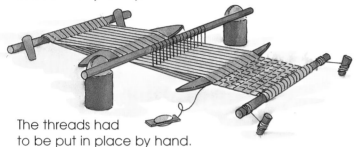

The threads had to be put in place by hand.

Weaving by hand was very slow. The **flying shuttle** was invented in 1733. It carried the thread from side to side automatically. Before this, it was passed through by hand.

The **Jacquard loom** was invented in 1801. It could weave complicated patterns into the cloth.

The loom was controlled by rows of holes in a long strip of card. Early computers used the same idea.

Rayon fibers, as seen under a powerful microscope.

The first **artificial fiber** was patented in 1892. It was an artificial silk, called rayon.

149

Thousands of years ago, people did not need to tell the time. They got up when the Sun rose and went to bed when it set. Gradually, as life became more complicated, clocks began to play a larger part in people's lives.

The first clocks were used for waking priests and monks in time for their nightly prayers. Today, clocks seem to rule our lives.

The first clocks were **shadow clocks**. The shadow moved as the Sun moved across the sky. They were invented around 3,500 years ago.

Mechanical clocks were probably developed in Europe during the 1200s. They did not have a face or hands, but rang bells.

The speed of the clock was controlled by a mechanism called an escapement, but it was not very accurate.

In a **water clock**, water drips out of a container so that the level of water inside gradually falls. The Ancient Egyptians were using water clocks about 1500 B.C.

The **pendulum clock** was invented in 1657. It was much more accurate than the clocks before it.

Each swing of the pendulum takes the same amount of time. This keeps the clock running at the same speed all the time.

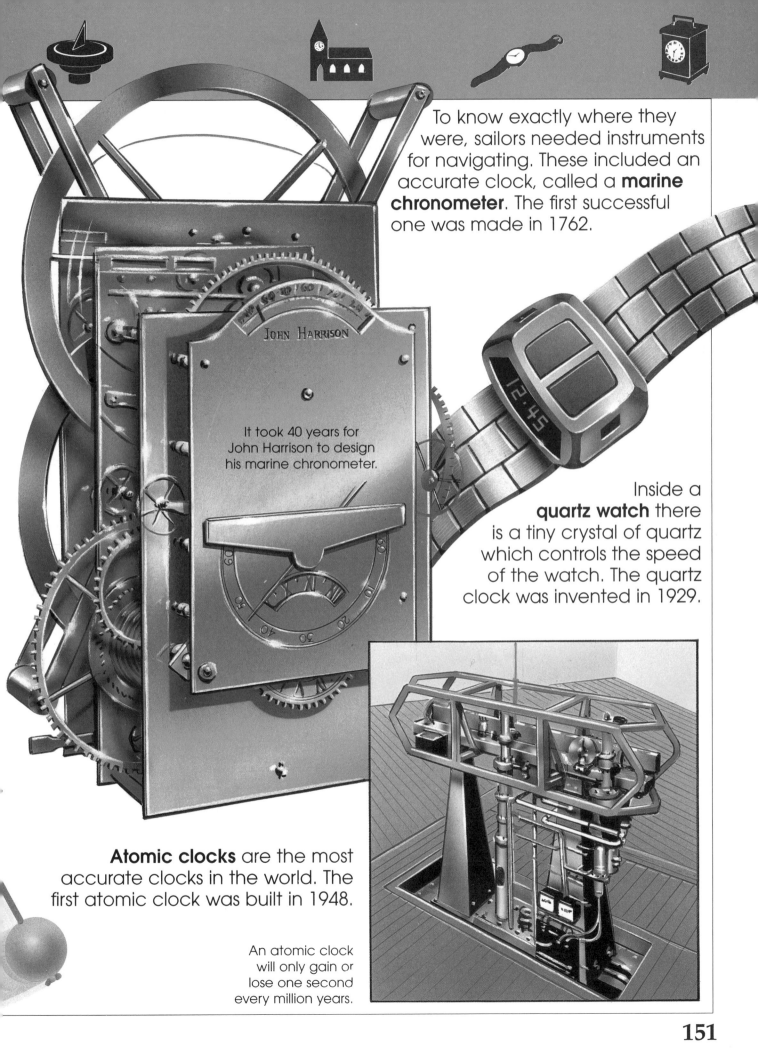

To know exactly where they were, sailors needed instruments for navigating. These included an accurate clock, called a **marine chronometer**. The first successful one was made in 1762.

JOHN HARRISON

It took 40 years for John Harrison to design his marine chronometer.

Inside a **quartz watch** there is a tiny crystal of quartz which controls the speed of the watch. The quartz clock was invented in 1929.

Atomic clocks are the most accurate clocks in the world. The first atomic clock was built in 1948.

An atomic clock will only gain or lose one second every million years.

Writing and printing

For thousands of years, people did not write anything down. Instead, they passed on information and stories by word of mouth. Shapes and pictures were the first sort of writing.

The books that we know today were not made until printing was invented. Until then, every book was copied by hand by people called scribes. Long books took months to copy.

The Ancient Egyptians used **picture writing**. Each small picture stood for a word or sound. These pictures, or symbols, are called hieroglyphics.

The first simple **pens** were brushes, or hollow reeds, dipped in ink. The Ancient Greeks used a metal, or bone, stylus to write on soft wax tablets. Later, people used quill pens made from goose feathers.

The end of a goose feather was sharpened and then cut to make a nib shape. To write with a quill, you have to keep dipping the nib in ink.

The first **ballpoint pens** were made in 1938 by Lazlo Biro. When a cheap ballpoint pen runs out, you throw it away. For other pens, you can buy an ink refill with a new ball.

Inside the tip of a ballpoint pen is a tiny steel ball. It rolls around as you write, spreading ink on to the paper.

The first **printed book** that still exists was made in China in 868. It is a long roll of paper, and is called the *Diamond Sutra*.

The *Diamond Sutra* was printed by pressing carved, wooden blocks covered with ink on to the paper.

Around 1450, Johannes Gutenberg built the first **printing press**. It could print about sixteen pages of a book every hour.

In 1939, **phototypesetting** was invented. It has now replaced metal type. The words are now typed onto a computer and printed out on photographic paper.

Gutenburg made up words by putting metal letters, called type, together.

Newspapers were first printed in Europe at the beginning of the 1600s. Before then, newspapers were only printed when there was a lot of news.

Listening to recorded music is something most people do every day. However, when sound recording was first invented it was a novelty, and nobody took it seriously.

Every so often, a new way of recording sound is invented. Recordings of speech and sounds are also important historical records.

The first machine to record sound and play it back was the **phonograph**. It was invented in 1877 by the American inventor Thomas Edison.

Speaking into the phonograph made a needle move up and down. As the drum went around, the needle made a groove in the tin foil.

A **tape recorder** records sound as a magnetic pattern on a long strand of tape. The first tape recorder used iron wire. Plastic tape coated with magnetic material appeared in 1935.

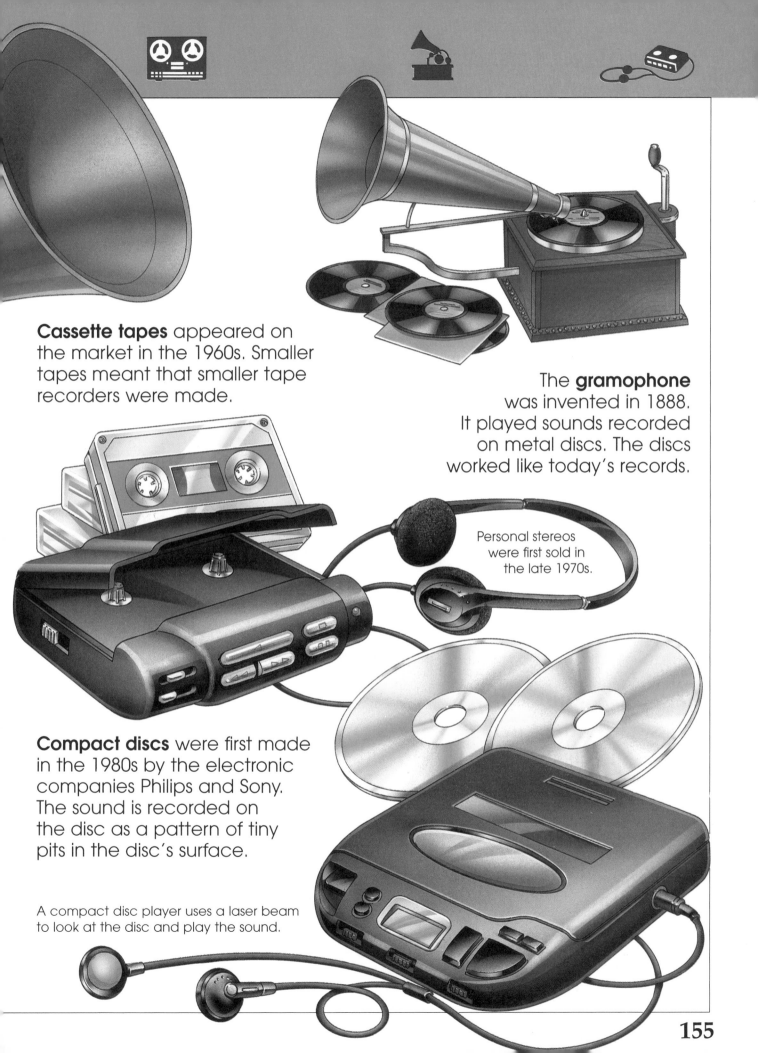

Cassette tapes appeared on the market in the 1960s. Smaller tapes meant that smaller tape recorders were made.

The **gramophone** was invented in 1888. It played sounds recorded on metal discs. The discs worked like today's records.

Personal stereos were first sold in the late 1970s.

Compact discs were first made in the 1980s by the electronic companies Philips and Sony. The sound is recorded on the disc as a pattern of tiny pits in the disc's surface.

A compact disc player uses a laser beam to look at the disc and play the sound.

The **semaphore** system was the first way of communicating over long distances. Semaphore stations were positioned on hilltops, and the message was passed from one station to the next. The system was first used in France in 1794.

The message was shown by moving the arms on top of the semaphore station to different positions.

Until about 200 years ago the only way to send a message was by messenger or by mail. Sometimes, hilltop bonfires were used to send emergency signals.

Today, you can talk on the telephone to friends and relations in almost any part of the world. It takes just a few seconds to dial. Your call might even travel via a satellite in space on the way.

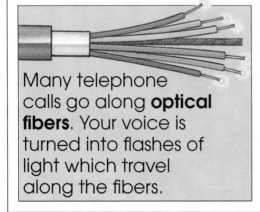

Many telephone calls go along **optical fibers**. Your voice is turned into flashes of light which travel along the fibers.

Messages were tapped with the key as dots and dashes.

The first simple electric **telegraph** was built in 1804. In 1837, Samuel Morse invented **Morse Code**. It was used to send messages by telegraph.

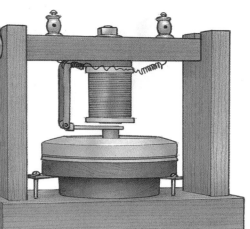

In 1876, Alexander Graham Bell patented the **telephone**. It converted sound into electrical signals. The signals were sent down a wire to another phone and turned back into sound.

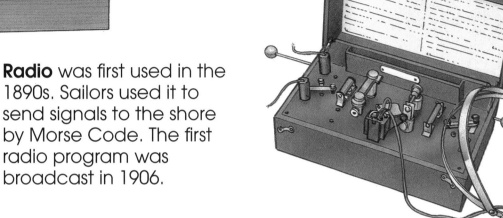

Radio was first used in the 1890s. Sailors used it to send signals to the shore by Morse Code. The first radio program was broadcast in 1906.

An automatic telephone exchange was in operation in 1897. **Electronic telephone exchanges** were built In the 1960s.

The first **telephone exchange** was built in 1878. Only a few people could use it, and it needed a person to operate it.

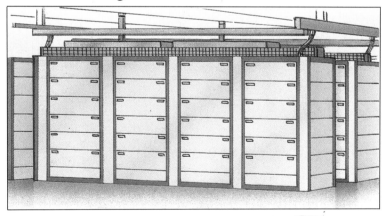

Facsimile machines (fax machines for short) send words and pictures along telephone lines. The idea for fax was first thought of in 1843, but it took until the 1980s for faxes to become common.

Until the 1820s there were no photographs or films. To make pictures of anything, people had to draw or paint them. Taking photographs is a much easier process.

When moving pictures first appeared nobody took them seriously. The machines that made the pictures move were thought of as toys.

Television is part of our everyday lives. We can watch soap operas, films, the news and sports. Thanks to satellites, we can even watch events happening live around the world.

The first **camera** of the type we use today was made by the Eastman company in 1888. It had film that you could send away for processing.

The **kinetoscope** was invented in 1891 by Thomas Edison. You had to look through the top and wind a handle. The film inside lasted only about 15 seconds.

Inside the kinetoscope was a long strip of film with hundreds of pictures on it. Each picture was slightly different from the one before to make an action sequence.

The first **cinema** opened in Paris in 1895. The film was projected on to a screen. The projector worked like the kinetoscope.

The first time **television** pictures were transmitted by electricity was in 1926. The pictures weren't very good - they were in black and white, wobbly and blurred.

The pattern of light and dark on the picture was made by a spinning disc with holes in it.

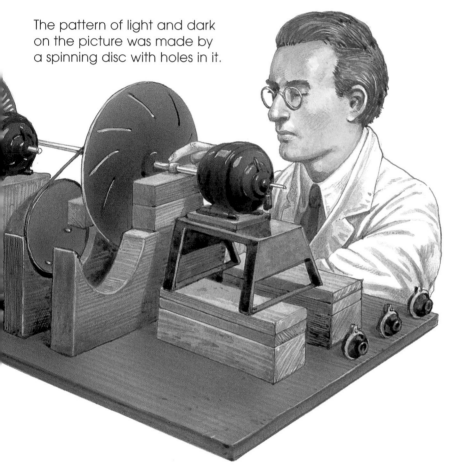

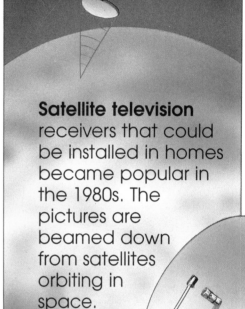

Satellite television receivers that could be installed in homes became popular in the 1980s. The pictures are beamed down from satellites orbiting in space.

In 1928, the first television program was broadcast In America. It was used to test a new **television transmitter**. The pictures were of Felix the Cat™.

Color television pictures were first broadcast in 1953.

Video tape and **video recorders** were invented in 1956. Pictures are recorded on videotape just as sounds are recorded on audio tape.

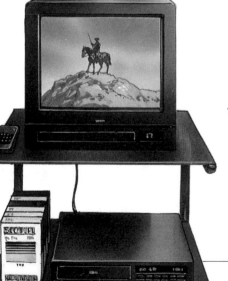

Electronic circuits are often used to control and work machines. Computers, televisions and telephones all use electronics. So do some simpler machines, such as washing machines and alarm clocks.

Electronic circuits are made up of electronic components. There are many different sorts of components. One of the most important is the transistor. Its invention meant that electronic circuits could be made much smaller than before.

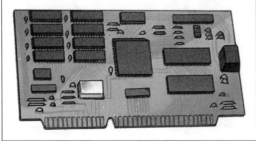

In the 1830s, years before electronics were possible, British scientist Charles Babbage designed a mechanical computer. He called it an **analytical engine**. It was never finished.

The first electronic device was called the **thermionic valve**. It was first made in 1904.

Thermionic valves were used in early radios and televisions.

The first general-purpose electronic **computer** was called ENIAC, which stands for Electronic Numerical Integrator and Calculator. It was built in 1946.

ENIAC used over 18,000 valves and filled a whole room.

The **transistor** was invented in 1948 by a team of scientists in America. Transistors took over from valves, but were much smaller and cheaper.

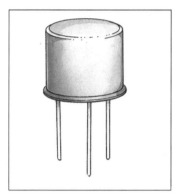

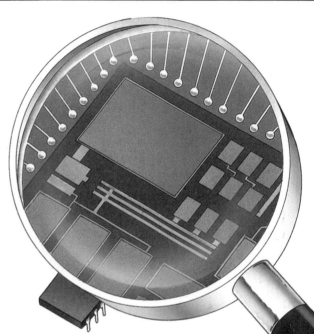

A **silicon chip**, or microchip, as small as a fingernail can contain many thousands of transistors and other electronic components. The first silicon chip was made in 1959.

A silicon chip in a plastic casing

Engineers began to fit more and more components on to a silicon chip. Eventually engineers at Intel built a complete computer on a single chip. This is called a **microprocessor**.

Every personal computer has a microprocessor "brain."

161

Until the eighteenth century people did all their household chores by hand. There were no washing machines or vacuum cleaners. No one had running water or a flushing toilet either.

The first domestic appliances were mechanical. It was still hard work to operate them. Things really changed when electric motors became cheap to make. Imagine what life today would be like without electricity!

A **flushing toilet** was invented by John Harington in 1589. The sort of toilet we use today first appeared at the end of the nineteenth century.

A Victorian wash-down water closet

Englishman Joseph Swan made a long-lasting **light bulb** in 1878. The next year, Thomas Edison made a similar bulb.

In Edison's light bulb, the electricity flowed through a piece of carbonized bamboo, making it glow.

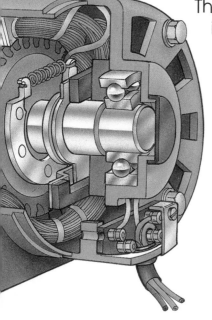

The first **electric motor** was made in 1835. Its power came from a battery because there was no mains electricity at the time.

Before refrigerators, food was kept fresh in a cool place or boxes lined with ice. The ice had to be replaced as it melted.

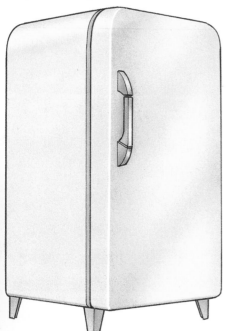

The **vacuum cleaner** was patented by Englishman Hubert Booth in 1901. Booth's first machine had to be hired, together with people to operate it.

Microwave ovens appeared in the 1950s. They were used by catering companies.

Refrigerating machines were developed at the end of the nineteenth century. It was not until the 1950s, however, that domestic refrigerators became popular.

Microwave ovens cook most foods many times faster than electric or gas ovens.

The existence of ghosts has never been proved scientifically. However throughout history many people have reported sightings of ghosts.

It is said that there have been many appearances of **royal ghosts.** King Henry VIII's beheaded wife, Anne Boleyn, is said to haunt the Tower of London, England. Two of his other wives roam the corridors at Hampton Court Palace.

Ghosts are believed to be the spirits of people who have died, but sometimes they seem to resemble living people. There are animal ghosts and even ghostly ships, cars, planes and trains.

In 1962, English brothers, Derek and Norman Ferguson claimed to have seen lots of **ghostly animals** while driving their car along a highway in Scotland.

A **bizarre bat** with a human head is a ghostly legend of Northern American Indians.

Haunted computers have been reported in many parts of the world.

Glamis Castle, the birthplace of Princess Margaret, is believed to be the most haunted royal building in Scotland. This 14th-century castle is said to be the home of a monster, a vampire and a whole host of ghosts.

Some people believe that ghosts like to haunt houses as well as ancient castles. In 1966, a British family had to be rehoused by their local government because they thought their house had been haunted for two years.

FOR SALE

Ghosts around the world

There have been hundreds of ghostly sightings. Such stories have been reported from many countries around the globe.

Often these stories reflect the legends and traditions of the country in which the hauntings occur.

One of the best known English ghosts is that of **Dick Turpin** who was famous for robbing travelers. He was a hero of the poor people because he stole from the wealthy. Turpin was hanged in 1739. It is widely believed that his ghost still appears on Hounslow Heath – now known as **Heathrow Airport**!

Abraham Lincoln was one of the most influential presidents of the United States. He was assassinated in April, 1865. It is said that every year during the month of April, the President's funeral train appears. It can be seen traveling along a stretch of track in New York State.

Over 150 years ago, a **Danish** man was wrongfully hanged for stealing. It is claimed that a shadowy outline of a body, hanging from a gallows, still appears today, just before the death of a family member.

It is said that whenever the President's ghostly train appears, a complete military band can be heard blasting away.

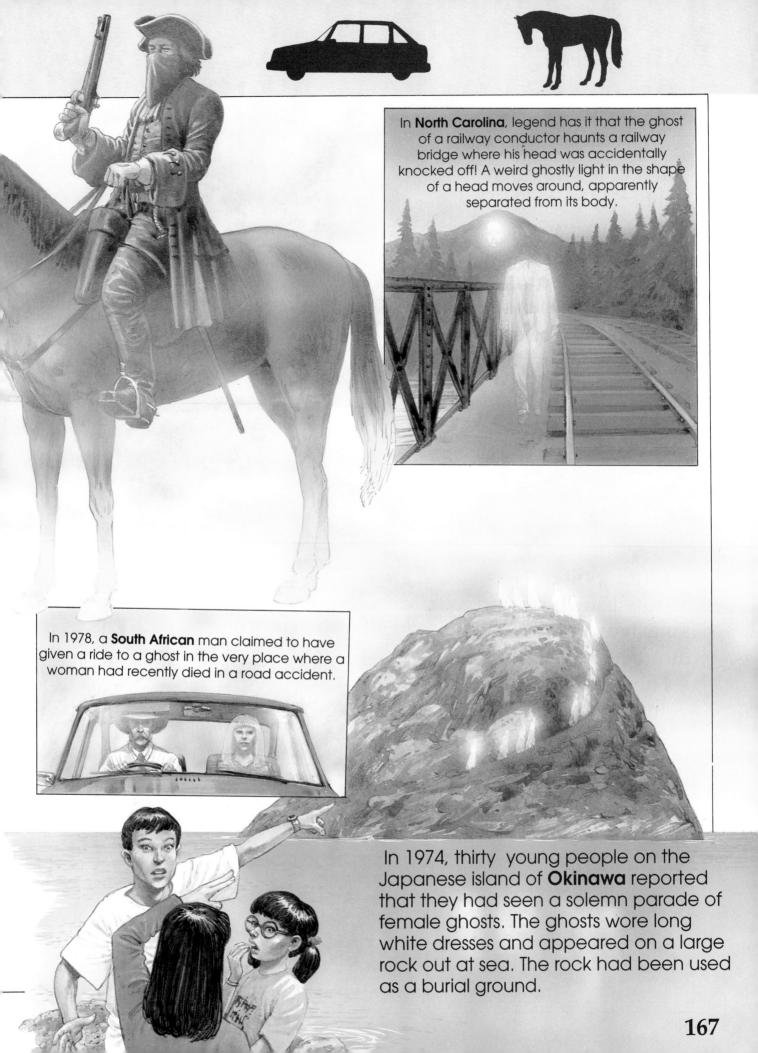

In **North Carolina**, legend has it that the ghost of a railway conductor haunts a railway bridge where his head was accidentally knocked off! A weird ghostly light in the shape of a head moves around, apparently separated from its body.

In 1978, a **South African** man claimed to have given a ride to a ghost in the very place where a woman had recently died in a road accident.

In 1974, thirty young people on the Japanese island of **Okinawa** reported that they had seen a solemn parade of female ghosts. The ghosts wore long white dresses and appeared on a large rock out at sea. The rock had been used as a burial ground.

167

Poltergeists

A poltergeist is described as an invisible and noisy ghost. It is said that when a poltergeist is present people hear scratching, banging and mysterious voices. Sometimes fires start and strange smells fill the air.

Often poltergeists throw things around, smash ornaments and move heavy furniture. They are said to be invisible vandals!

In 1661, a magistrate confiscated a drum from a local beggar in **Tedworth**, England. Legend has it that a phantom drum could be heard frequently and lit candles floated up the chimney. The magistrate's horse was even found with its hind leg stuck in its mouth!

A family in **Barbados** buried deceased relatives in a big tomb. Each time the tomb was opened the coffins were found scattered around.

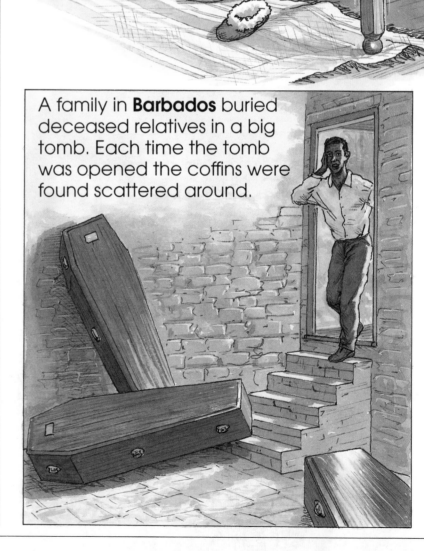

In 1960, an 11-year-old Scottish girl, **Virginia Campbell**, claimed she was being aggravated by a poltergeist for two months. It followed her wherever she went. One night her bed started shaking as if there was an earthquake. The haunting stopped once her parents held prayer meetings in their house.

Objects were said to fly around when a poltergeist made its home on a farm in **Lancashire**, England. A cow was even lifted to a hay loft. How it got there nobody knows – it certainly could not have climbed up the rickety ladder.

In 1951, a family reported strange happenings in their **London** home. A policeman found furniture being thrown across a room. Strangely, the violent activity stopped instantly once a light was turned on.

During 1967, a poltergeist started creating a disruption around 11-year-old **Matthew Manning** from Cambridge, England. Furniture began to move all over the family home and strange scratching noises could be heard. The haunting ended when Matthew began to create strange and beautiful drawings.

169

Funny ghosts

It is said that ghosts like playing tricks. But ghosts and people seem to have a very different sense of humor. Often people do not find what ghosts do very funny. Ghosts are more likely to terrify people than make them laugh.

Over 60 years ago, on the Isle of Man in the Irish Sea, a ghostly **mongoose** was said to haunt an old farmhouse by the sea. It told jokes, sang songs and even swore. It told everyone its name was Gef. When the farmhouse was sold the new owner shot an unusual little furry animal. Gef has never been seen since.

Over 25 years ago, a derelict hotel in Wales was being demolished. Even though the electricity to the building had been cut off, the **elevator** kept on working.

Twelve-year-old English boy, **Michael Collingridge**, was recovering from tonsillitis when a walking stick in his bedroom appeared to dance. It jumped all around the room and began to tap out well-known tunes!

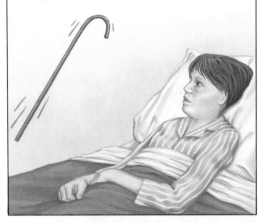

When the Pritchard family from **Pontefract** in Wales was plagued by a ghost, a woman from a Christian charity tried to drive the ghost away by singing *Onward Christian Soldiers*. The ghost responded by picking up her gloves and conducting her as she sang!

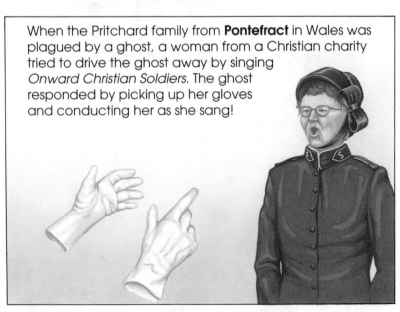

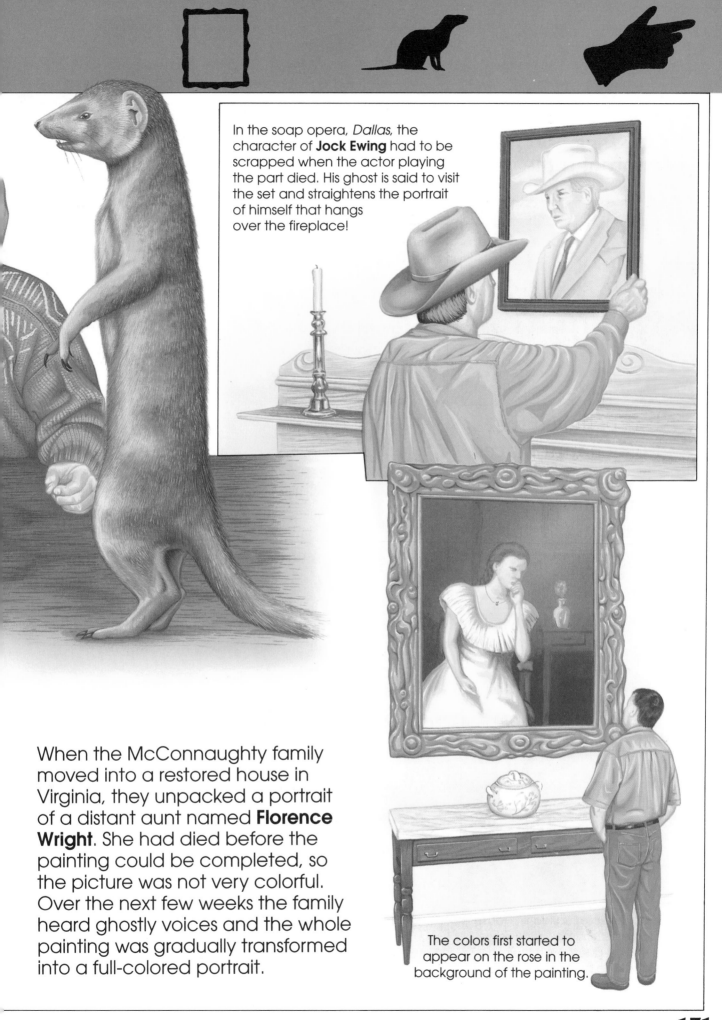

In the soap opera, *Dallas,* the character of **Jock Ewing** had to be scrapped when the actor playing the part died. His ghost is said to visit the set and straightens the portrait of himself that hangs over the fireplace!

When the McConnaughty family moved into a restored house in Virginia, they unpacked a portrait of a distant aunt named **Florence Wright**. She had died before the painting could be completed, so the picture was not very colorful. Over the next few weeks the family heard ghostly voices and the whole painting was gradually transformed into a full-colored portrait.

The colors first started to appear on the rose in the background of the painting.

Haunted houses

It is said that haunted houses creak and ghosts glide through the walls.

It is believed that ghosts haunt places where they once lived, but no one knows if hauntings really happen!

Legend has it that **Ballechin House** in Scotland is haunted by invisible dogs who hit guests with their tails. It is also said to be home to ghostly nuns and a disembodied hand!

Raynham Hall in Norfolk, England, is thought to be haunted by the ghost of Dorothy Walpole who died there. In 1936, a photograph of a ghostly woman in a veil was snapped by a professional photographer visiting the hall.

After studying the picture, some experts believe that it is genuine.

The most haunted house in Britain was said to be **Borley Rectory**. Even though it burnt down in 1939, poltergeists are said to haunt the ruins. Two headless ghosts and a phantom nun are also believed to have appeared.

The home of the British Prime Minister, **Number 10 Downing Street**, London, is said to be haunted by a politician from regency times.

Between 1883 and 1934, number **16 Montpelier Road** in London was the scene of twenty suicides and one murder. The victims had fallen from the top of the tower. In 1944, an investigator visited the house and was almost thrown from the tower himself. A photograph taken shows a ghost in Victorian clothing in an upstairs window!

Scaring away ghosts

People have invented all kinds of weird ways to ward off ghosts. Good luck charms and complicated rituals are used to scare ghosts away.

Inuits never remove someone who has died in an **igloo** through the front door. It is thought the spirit of the dead person would return if it knew where the front door was!

In China, the burning of **joss sticks** is thought to ward off unwanted spirits. Loud drums are beaten and noisy fireworks are set off at funerals to frighten away evil spirits.

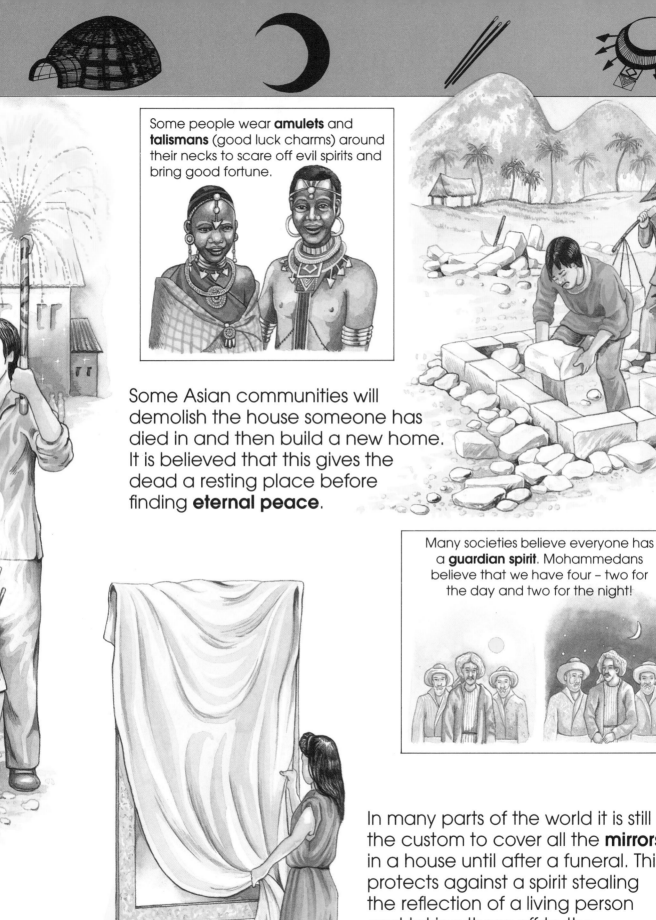

Some people wear **amulets** and **talismans** (good luck charms) around their necks to scare off evil spirits and bring good fortune.

Some Asian communities will demolish the house someone has died in and then build a new home. It is believed that this gives the dead a resting place before finding **eternal peace**.

Many societies believe everyone has a **guardian spirit**. Mohammedans believe that we have four – two for the day and two for the night!

In many parts of the world it is still the custom to cover all the **mirrors** in a house until after a funeral. This protects against a spirit stealing the reflection of a living person and taking them off to the spirit world.

Throughout history there have been reports of people vanishing without trace. Ships and airplanes seem to have disappeared into thin air! Some of these cases are still shrouded in mystery.

Sometimes stories have been made up to explain disappearances. When famous band leader, **Glenn Miller**, vanished in 1944, some people believed that his face had been so disfigured in a plane crash that he had decided to hide away for the rest of his life.

The crew's meal was found half-eaten on the table.

In 1872, the entire crew of the merchant ship, the *Marie Celeste*, vanished. The ship was completely undamaged but no one aboard was ever seen again.

Often disappearances are hoaxes. In 1880, the story of a farmer who had apparently vanished hit the headlines in **Tennessee**. It turned out that a hardware salesman, who had been snowed into his house, had invented the whole story out of boredom!

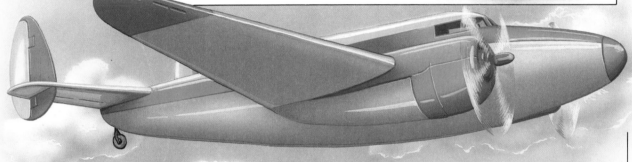

In 1937, **Amelia Earhart**, a record-breaking pilot, disappeared en route to an island in the Pacific Ocean. No one has ever been able to explain this mysterious disappearance.

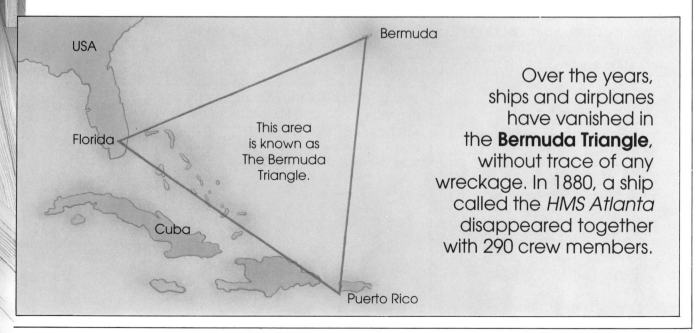

USA

Bermuda

Florida

This area is known as The Bermuda Triangle.

Cuba

Puerto Rico

Over the years, ships and airplanes have vanished in the **Bermuda Triangle**, without trace of any wreckage. In 1880, a ship called the *HMS Atlanta* disappeared together with 290 crew members.

Witchcraft

Witchcraft comes from two old English words, *wita* and *craeft* which means craft of the wise. Some witches are thought to have special knowledge of the plants and herbs used to cure sickness.

In the past witches were thought to use their powers in an evil way.

In the past, anybody accused of **witchcraft** could be brought to trial. They were sometimes tortured until they had no option but to "confess."

Witchcraft was outlawed in the United Kingdom until 1951, when the old law was overturned. Today, it is quite legal to be a witch and join a **coven** or group of witches.

During 1692, in **Salem**, Massachusetts, a group of children accused 200 residents of being witches. The "witches" were brought to trial and 20 were executed. It was later agreed it had all been a terrible mistake.

At the time of the **winter solstice**, in December, witches perform "The Dance of the Wheel," a special ceremony to coax back the sun. They dance and leap around a boiling cauldron to represent the spring.

Traditional doctors in Africa used to be referred to as **witch doctors.** These doctors are expert herbalists and they sometimes call upon spirit powers to help cure their patients.

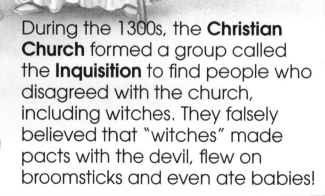

During the 1300s, the **Christian Church** formed a group called the **Inquisition** to find people who disagreed with the church, including witches. They falsely believed that "witches" made pacts with the devil, flew on broomsticks and even ate babies!

179

Fortune telling

Many people believe that fortunetellers can look into the future. Some of them look at cards or tea leaves. Others look to the stars to see what lies ahead.

Rune stones are a set of 25 small tablets or stones which are believed to have special meaning. A rune reader can recognize what the stones represent according to the way they are laid out.

Most fortune telling methods originated in China. **I Ching** is an ancient Chinese book of knowledge which is believed to have the answer to everything!

No two hands are the same. **Palmists** read people's hands to predict how long they will live and even how many children they will have.

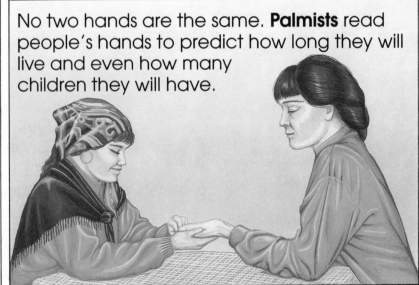

Astrology places people into twelve different groups which correspond with their birth dates. Maps of the stars and planets are consulted to forecast what the future holds.

Phrenology is the art of telling a fortune by feeling the bumps on a person's head.

Some people read their **horoscope** to predict what will happen during a day, week or month.

The Chinese invented **dominoes** as a method of predicting the future. The dominoes are put in a pouch, shaken and removed. Fortunes are read according to the position in which the dominoes are laid out.

Second sight

Some people claim to have second sight. They believe that they see or sense things which are invisible to other people. Sometimes they even say that they can tell when a terrible event is about to happen.

In 1889, **Morgan Roberts** wrote *The Wreck of the Titan*. It tells the story of a massive luxury liner, called the *Titan*, which hit an iceberg and sank. The ***Titanic*** did exactly that 14 years later and hundreds of the passengers were drowned.

In 1925, a famous palmist predicted that **Edward, Prince of Wales** would be forced to abdicate soon after he became King. Amazingly, 11 years later this premonition became fact!

In May 1979, an American called **David Booth** dreamed of a terrible air crash. He informed the airline but they took no notice of him. The next day an airplane crashed at the Chicago airport killing 273 people.

Jeane Dixon, an American who claims to have powers of second sight, warned that the President would be assassinated. Eventually, on November 23, 1963, she told friends that the day had come.
John F. Kennedy was shot dead that afternoon.

The police have often been helped by people with second sight. **Gerald Croiset** spent his life helping Danish police to find murderers and to locate missing people and buried bodies.

Amazing powers

It is said that some people are gifted with bizarre powers. They claim to be able to make things rise above the ground and objects change shape all by themselves.

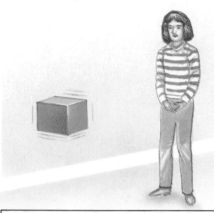

Astral projection is when a person feels that their spirit is rising out of their actual body. Such people claim that while sleeping they can sit on the end of their bed and watch themselves.

Many people believe that **dowsers** can sense where gold and oil are hidden in the ground. They use instruments, such as bent metal rods or forked twigs, which tremble or rotate when they have found the hidden treasure.

Levitation is said to defy the law of gravity by making bodies or objects rise and float in the air. Some eastern holy men are supposed to be able to levitate themselves at will.

Experts are unable to explain the strange pictures created by psychic photography.

It is claimed that **psychic photography** is the ability to take photographs of thoughts. Ted Serios from Chicago believed that when he took a photograph of his face an image in his thoughts would appear on the film!

Psychokinesis is the ability to affect objects by mental means alone. **Uri Geller** from Israel, for example, is famous for bending keys. He has even claimed to be able to stop a cable car in midair. Many magicians believe he is a fraud.

Strange and bizarre

For hundreds of years sightings of strange creatures, mysterious monsters and bizarre landmarks have been reported all over the world. Even today experts are unable to find scientific explanations for many of these mysteries.

Bigfoot – or Sasquatch – is described as a tall, hairy monster that lives in Washington State. A Bigfoot sighting is reported regularly so there must be lots of these monsters!

Yeti, or the **Abominable Snowman** is thought to be a tall, white, furry monster. The first sighting was reported in Tibet in 1921 and there have been numerous reports of appearances ever since.

Enormous, elaborate shapes known as **crop circles** have appeared in the crop fields of Hampshire and Wiltshire, England. No one is sure how they are formed or where they came from although many explanations have been suggested.

It is said that the **Pyramids** in Egypt are surrounded by strange powers. Plants apparently grow faster and it is even claimed that people are filled with amazing energy around the Pyramids!

Nowadays modern technology, from radar to the latest computers, is used to investigate sightings of unknown creatures.

The **Loch Ness Monster** is believed to be a gigantic prehistoric reptile which still survives in Loch Ness, Scotland. Sightings of it have been reported as long ago as 565 B.C. Although there are numerous photographs, the existence of this "monster" has never really been proved.

More spooky cases

Tradition has it that when a dramatic event has occurred, ghostly phantoms will return to haunt the place where the disturbing incident happened.

Here are two especially chilling phantom stories.

During the 1600s, the owner of **Bettiscombe Manor** in Dorset, England cruelly enslaved an African man and brought him back to England. The slave said that if he was not buried in his homeland he would return to haunt the manor. The slave's request was ignored and he was buried in the local churchyard.

It is said that such terrible screaming could be heard in the churchyard that the owner was forced to dig up the coffin and put it in the loft of Bettiscombe Manor.

The skull remains at Bettiscombe Manor and seems to guard it. If the skull is taken outside, it is said that screams shake the house.

The Flying Dutchman was a ship which sank in the 1600s. Its ghost is said to haunt the oceans. In 1881, the crew of *HMS Inconstant* thought they saw the ship.

In 1939, over 100 people claimed to have seen the ship as they sunbathed on a beach near Cape Town, South Africa.

During World War II, a German admiral reported that the crew of his U-Boat submarine had seen the phantom ship.

In 1911, the crew of the steamer, *Orkney Belle*, encountered **The Flying Dutchman**. It was totally deserted. It is said that three bells were heard and the ghost ship vanished into the fog.

Index

ISBN 0-590-39772-9

Copyright © 1995 by Zigzag Publishing Ltd.
All rights reserved. Published by Scholastic Inc., 555 Broadway, New York, NY 10012, by arrangement with Zigzag Publishing Ltd.

SCHOLASTIC and associated logos are trademarks and/or registered trademarks of Scholastic Inc.

12 11 10 9 8 7 6 5 4 3 2 1   8 9/9 0 1 2/0

Printed in the U.S.A.   14
First Scholastic printing, January 1998